For Lachlan and Dylan
whose integrity and commitment inspire me every day.

And to all sports officials - those who stand up, step up, and show up - thank you for your courage, resilience, and unwavering dedication to the game.

FROM THE AUTHOR

Welcome to *The Whistle Blower*, a mental toughness rulebook created for the referees, umpires, and officials who make sports possible. This book recognizes the essential role you play—and the unique mental challenges you face—performing under the constant scrutiny of athletes, coaches, and fans. Within these pages, you'll find practical strategies, real-world insights, and support for thriving in the heart of the action, because your resilience and presence are at the very core of every game.

The championship game is always the highlight. So much hard work, strategy, and effort culminate in these final moments, with everything on the line for ultimate glory. The crowd settles in, the energy builds—everyone is ready for the contest. The players line up, anticipation on their faces, waiting for the opening whistle. And then, the final essential members of the event take their positions: the officials.

This scene unfolds in stadiums and parks across America, from the bright lights of the NFL and NBA to neighborhood baseball diamonds and high school gyms. While the spotlight often shines on players and coaches, it's the referees and umpires who stand at the heart of every contest—often unnoticed, sometimes criticized, but always indispensable. Without you, the game simply doesn't happen.

I've spent much of my life on the sidelines and in the thick of the action—first as a young coach, then as an official, and later as a mentor and advocate for sports officials across many codes. My journey began at fifteen, when I was entrusted with coaching a netball team. I quickly learned that the whistle was as much a part of the game as any pass or shot. It was a lesson in humility, resilience, and the quiet courage required to make decisions under pressure.

Those early experiences shaped my understanding of the unique pressures faced by referees and umpires. I remember the nerves before my first big game, the weight of expectation from coaches and parents, and the knowledge that every decision would be scrutinized. The championship, in particular, was a challenge—an arena where the stakes were high and the margin for error slim. Yet, it was also where I learned the most about myself: about composure, fairness, and the importance of community.

Years later, as a parent, I found myself once again on the edge of the field, this time watching one of my sons take up the whistle for his first championship game. The crowd was smaller, the stakes different, but my anticipation was far higher than anything I'd felt watching the National Rugby League Grand Final on TV the day before. As he took his place in the middle of the field, I sat under the trees, camera at the ready, watching with one eye half-shut! Nothing quite describes the feeling of watching your child stand alone, under the spotlight and the scrutiny of others. Would he be okay? Would he take criticism? What if he made a mistake?

What set my mind at ease was what happened at halftime. While the players took a well-earned break, the three officials gathered at midfield and were immediately joined by other referees who had been quietly watching from the sidelines—offering encouragement, feedback, and, most importantly, reminding the young officials that they were not alone. Did they make mistakes? Probably. But as with everything, it's not whether we make mistakes, but whether we learn from them that matters.

This moment crystallized for me why I am so passionate about supporting referees, umpires, and officials. Officiating can be a thankless job. As one league executive once said, "It's not possible to avoid errors. Errors, by their very definition, aren't intended to happen." No one takes the field or court intending to make a mistake. Yet, in the aftermath of high-stakes games, it's often the officials who become the focal point of criticism and debate. The "six to go" controversy in Australia's NRL Grand Final—a rugby league equivalent to the Super Bowl—dominated headlines not by the players' feats, but by the officials' split-second decisions.

My motivation for writing *The Whistle Blower* is deeply personal. I've been privileged to work with officials from a wide range of sports—football, basketball, baseball, netball, and more. I've seen firsthand the dedication, integrity, and resilience required to officiate at every level, from youth leagues to the pros. I've also witnessed the toll that criticism and abuse can take—not just on individuals, but on the entire sporting community.

Officials are the guardians of the game's spirit. You uphold the rules, ensure fairness, and provide a safe environment for athletes to compete. Your decisions shape the flow of play and, ultimately, the outcome. Yet, your contribution is often overlooked—until something goes wrong.

Through this book, I aim to shine a light on the world of sports officiating: the challenges, the rewards, and the human experience behind the whistle. I want to explore what it takes to make decisions under pressure, to bounce back from mistakes, and to find joy in a role that is as demanding as it is vital.

For those who support officials—parents, coaches, administrators, and fans—I hope this book will foster greater understanding and empathy. The next time you find yourself questioning a call, remember the courage it takes to make that call in real time, with the eyes of the crowd upon you.

To all referees, umpires, and officials: thank you for the community you provide and for giving our athletes the opportunity to play. Your presence makes the game possible.

Play on, Dr. Jo

CONTENTS

Introduction   1
Stepping into the Spotlight

PART 1
LAYING THE GROUNDWORK FOR SUCCESS

Rule 1   7
Pre-Game Playbook

Rule 1.1   9
Own Your Preparation—The Winning Edge

Rule 1.2   14
Inspect and Prepare—The Devil is in the Details

Rule 1.3   18
Visualize Success—Mind Over Matter

Rule 1 in Summary   22
The Pre-Game Playbook Rule

Rule 2   25
Mind and Body in Sync

Rule 2.1   27
Sleep Like a Champion—Rest for Success

Rule 2.2   31
Peak Fitness for Peak Performance—The Physical Edge

Rule 2.3   35
Fuel Your Mind—Nutrition for Excellence

Rule 2 in Summary   39
The Mind and Body in Sync Rule

Rule 3   42
Master Your Time

Rule 3.1   44
Arrive Early, Leave Later—The Time Advantage

Rule 3.2   48
Learn from the Past, Stay in the Present, Be Ready for the Future—Timeless Wisdom

Rule 3.3 *Plan for Overtime Before it Happens—Anticipate and Adapt*	54
Rule 3 in Summary *The Master Your Time Rule*	59

PART 2
THE MENTAL PILLARS OF PERFORMANCE

Rule 4 *The Power of the Whistle*	65
Rule 4.1 *Control What You Can, Accept What You Can't—The Art of Letting Go*	67
Rule 4.2 *Think Before You Act—Consequences of Each Call*	72
Rule 4.3 *Influence Through Presence—Your Body Speaks First*	78
Rule 4 in Summary *The Power of the Whistle Rule*	83
Rule 5 *Split-Second Clarity*	86
Rule 5.1 *Trust Your Instincts—The Power of Decision Conviction*	88
Rule 5.2 *Mindful Presence—Being in the Moment*	93
Rule 5.3 *Focus and Process—The Art of Mental Filtering*	97
Rule 5 in Summary *The Split-Second Clarity Rule*	102
Rule 6 *Command, Connect, and Focus*	105
Rule 6.1 *Clear and Confident Communication—The Voice of Authority*	107
Rule 6.2 *Nonverbal Communication—The Unspoken Language*	113
Rule 6.3 *Adaptive Communication—Flexibility in Action*	118
Rule 6 in Summary *The Command, Connect, and Focus Rule*	122

PART 3
MENTAL RESILIENCE

Rule 7 *Discover Your Inner Coach*	127
Rule 7.1 *Positive Self-Talk—The Power of Helpful Thinking*	129
Rule 7.2 *Constructive Self-Reflection—Learning from Experience*	134
Rule 7.3 *Mental Reset Techniques—Regain Your Focus*	139
Rule 7 in Summary *The Discover Your Inner Coach Rule*	143
Rule 8 *The Bounce-Back Blueprint*	146
Rule 8.1 *Rapid Mental Rebound Technique—Quick Recovery*	148
Rule 8.2 *Building Mental Resilience—The Long Game*	152
Rule 8.3 *Mental Recovery During Breaks—Recharge and Refocus*	157
Rule 8 in Summary *The Bounce-Back Blueprint Rule*	162
Rule 9 *Pressure Points*	165
Rule 9.1 *Emotional Control—Staying Calm Under Fire*	167
Rule 9.2 *Composure Techniques—Keeping Your Cool*	171
Rule 9.3 *Pressure as Opportunity—Turning Stress into Strength*	175
Rule 9 in Summary *The Pressure Points Rule*	179

PART 4
GROWTH AND DEVELOPMENT

Rule 10 *Reflect and Grow*	185
Rule 10.1 *Systematic Self-Evaluation—The Path to Progress*	187
Rule 10.2 *Progress Tracking and Celebration—Measuring Success*	192

Rule 10.3 *Feedback and Sharing—Learning from Others*	196
Rule 10 in Summary *The Reflect and Grow Rule*	200
Rule 11 *Strength in Numbers*	203
Rule 11.1 *Building Relationships—The Power of Community*	205
Rule 11.2 *Mentorship and Learning—Passing on Wisdom*	210
Rule 11.3 *Community Support—Standing Together*	214
Rule 11 in Summary *The Strength in Numbers Rule*	218
Rule 12 *Thriving in Officiating*	221
Rule 12.1 *Cultivating Curiosity—The Mind of a Learner*	223
Rule 12.2 *Practicing Gratitude—Finding Positivity*	228
Rule 12.3 *Continuous Learning and Growth—The Journey Never Ends*	232
Bonus Rule *Holistic Well-Being—Balancing Life and Sport*	236
Rule 12 in Summary *The Thrive in Officiating Rule*	240
Conclusion *Elevating Excellence in Officiating*	243
Bonus offer *Winning at Wellbeing: The Mental Fitness Blueprint*	247
About Dr. Jo	249
A Note from Dr. Jo	251
Stay connected with Dr. Jo	253
Read more with Dr. Jo	254

INTRODUCTION
STEPPING INTO THE SPOTLIGHT

Imagine standing in the center of a roaring stadium, whistle in hand, as thousands of eyes scrutinize your every move. The weight of the game rests on your shoulders, and in a split second, you must make a decision that could change everything. This is the world of sports officiating, where mental toughness isn't just an advantage—it's a necessity.

For many, the path to becoming a referee or umpire starts in their teenage years. It often begins with a deep love for the game and a nudge from coaches or mentors to gain that coveted level-one accreditation. What starts as a way to stay connected to a loved sport can quickly evolve into something much more rewarding.

As you progress, you may find that officiating offers unique rewards, including the rush of athleticism whilst guiding the game, the challenge of split-second decision-making, and the opportunity to engage with sport at higher levels.

For some, refereeing remains a part-time passion that complements their athletic journey. For others, it becomes their primary sporting pursuit. And for an elite few, it transforms into a full-fledged profession.

But no matter where you are on this continuum, one thing is clear: you've recognized the critical importance of the mental game in officiating excellence. You've taken a crucial step toward elevating your performance by picking up this book. You now understand that the sharpness of your mind is just as important as the sharpness of your whistle.

In the following pages, we'll explore the psychological tools and techniques that separate good officials from great ones.

We'll delve into:
- strategies for maintaining focus under pressure
- techniques for managing on-field conflicts
- methods for building unshakeable confidence

Unlike generic mental toughness resources, this rulebook speaks directly to the experiences and needs of sports officials. The architecture is built for optimal learning and implementation, perfect for quick study or pre-game mental preparation. The quick-reference design allows you to easily revisit specific rules when you need them most, while official-centric examples demonstrate real-world scenarios that resonate with your experiences on the field or court. It also follows a progressive skill building format, designed to help you develop your mental toughness systematically as you work your way through.

The book is organized into four parts and contains 12 rules. Each rule contains three sub-rules, where we deep dive into the concepts, exploring why they matter (The Call), the benefits to be gained (The Advantage), the risks of not adopting them (The Penalty), and practical ways to introduce the concepts into your officiating (The Game Plan).

Additionally, there is an accompanying workbook designed to help you dive deeper into each rule. You can download a free electronic copy, or, if you prefer a physical edition, The Whistle Blower Workbook is available to you at a special price.

How to Use This Guide

1. Read the entire rulebook from cover to cover, to grasp the full range of mental toughness skills.
2. Then focus on one rule at a time, implementing the application exercises in your training and matches.
3. Use the quick-reference format to reinforce specific skills before challenging games or tournaments.
4. Revisit the rulebook regularly to refine your mental approach and address new challenges.

As a sports official, you face unique situations that demand exceptional mental fortitude. Embrace this rulebook as your trusted companion in the pursuit of officiating excellence. With each page, you'll unlock new dimensions of mental resilience, equipping yourself to thrive under pressure and elevate the integrity of your sport.

Remember, your performance as a referee directly reflects your mental skills. The decisions you make, the composure you maintain, and the respect you command all stem from the strength of your mind. So, whether you're just starting or a seasoned professional, prepare to embark on a journey that will transform how you officiate and approach challenges in all aspects of life.

Welcome to the world of mental toughness for referees—where the most important calls are the ones you make inside your head. This book is your compass, designed to navigate the complex terrain of officiating with clarity and precision.

Let's get started.

PART 1
LAYING THE GROUNDWORK FOR SUCCESS

"THE KEY TO SUCCESS AS A SPORTING OFFICIAL IS LATE NIGHTS, JUNK FOOD, arriving at the last minute, and not getting too caught up in training, stretching, or revising the rules." As I uttered these words to a group of referees at a recent presentation, a wave of reactions swept across the room. Eyebrows raised in surprise, brows furrowed in confusion, and I could almost hear the unspoken questions about the sanity of the organizers who had invited me to speak. The palpable tension in the air was exactly what I had hoped for.

Of course, nothing could be further from the truth. While it may not be the most glamorous aspect of officiating, the foundation of high performance lies in mastering all the little things—the unglamorous, often overlooked details that separate good officials from great ones. Establishing your foundations and preparations will prepare you for the competition and give you confidence before the match commences.

Within Part I, we will consider the foundations of building your mental toughness journey:

Rule 1: Pre-Game Preparation

Knowing you've covered all bases before the first whistle blows, you can confidently step onto the field.

Rule 2: Mind and Body in Sync

Explains how to align your mind and body so you are ready to tackle any challenge the game presents.

Rule 3: Master Your Time

To help you master the art of time management, using it as your ally to navigate through every match with precision and control.

Many of these concepts may already be familiar, but when applied well, their benefits are significant. Even elite referees spend more time on the fundamentals than you might expect. Just like the referees in the room that day, when I asked them to correct my poor advice, they identified all the rules you'll find in Part 1. While we all know these foundations, the real challenge is how consistently we put them into practice. Once you have these foundational skills, you pave the way to benefit more from all of the other mental skills.

Remember: Success in officiating isn't just about what you do during the game—it's about the foundation you build before it begins.

RULE 1
PRE-GAME PLAYBOOK

"One important key to success is self-confidence. An important key to self-confidence is preparation."
—Arthur Ashe

JAKE BOUNCED THE BALL AT CENTER COURT, SCANNING THE lines and checking his watch, a familiar mix of excitement and nerves swirling in his stomach. The buzz of the arena energized him, but a few butterflies lingered, reminding him of the pressure ahead. As tip-off approached, Jake knew his pregame routine would not only settle those jitters but also give him the confidence he needed to referee at his best.

Two key elements that emerge from these discussions are the sense of readiness and the feeling of control that thorough preparation provides. While each game and competition brings unique challenges and unexpected situations, *the perception and feeling* of being well-prepared helps reduce anxiety and increase confidence.

Within Rule 1, we will explore the concept of preparation and how it fundamentally impacts your officiating performance.

Rule 1.1: Own Your Preparation—The Winning Edge
Rule 1.2: Inspect and Prepare—The Devil is in the Details
Rule 1.3: Visualize Success—Mind Over Matter

This mental rule emphasizes the importance of a comprehensive pre-game routine. Mastering your preparation lays the foundation for confident and effective officiating, ensuring you step onto the field or court ready to handle the game's challenges.

RULE 1.1

OWN YOUR PREPARATION—THE WINNING EDGE

The Call

As a referee, your game doesn't start when you step onto the playing arena. It starts hours before, in your mind, and through your actions. Feeling in control, connected, and capable are basic psychological needs. Your pre-game routine is your chance to nail all three.

Think of it as setting the stage for your performance. You're priming yourself for success like an actor rehearsing lines or an athlete visualizing their moves. This isn't about superstition—it's about creating a mental and physical state that allows you to perform at your peak.

Have you ever shown up to a competition distracted, unsure, or feeling unprepared? That's a recipe for sub-optimal performance. Your pre-game routine is your secret weapon to confidence and being ready. It's how you show up as the best version of yourself, ready to make those tough calls with conviction.

Consistency is key here. Establishing a routine creates a sense of normalcy and control, even in high-pressure situations. Whether it's a pickup game or a grand final, consistency in the pre-game routine is key. This familiarity can be a powerful anchor when the game gets intense. Plus, a solid routine helps you transition from your everyday life into your role as an official, getting you into the right headspace to manage the game effectively.

The Advantage

Nailing your pre-game preparation is like sharpening your competitive edge. Here's what you gain:

☑ *A major confidence boost*: You'll enter the field knowing you're ready for anything.

☑ *Laser-sharp focus when it counts*: Your mind is clear and focused on the task.

☑ *Less stress and fewer game-day jitters*: A routine helps calm those pre-game nerves.

☑ *A performance edge*: Preparation often separates good officials from great ones.

☑ *Long-term growth*: Consistent preparation habits contribute to continuous improvement.

A well-executed pre-game routine can enhance your decision-making abilities. When you're prepared, you'll likely make quick, accurate calls under pressure. This preparedness also translates into better communication with players, coaches, and fellow officials, leading to smoother game management.

The Penalty

Insufficient preparation casts a long shadow over an official's performance, resulting in many mental and physical challenges. As the whistle blows and the game unfolds, the unprepared official may grapple with worry, their decision-making abilities compromised in the heat of crucial moments. The mind, lacking the anchor of thorough preparation, may wander, struggling to maintain the laser-like focus required to track the play and apply rules with precision. Perhaps of most concern, the gnawing awareness of being underprepared can erode self-confidence, leading to hesitation when split-second calls are required.

The body, too, bears the brunt of inadequate preparation. Skipping proper warm-up routines is not merely a less disciplined approach, but a gamble with your physical well-being. The risk of strain or injury looms larger when you step onto the field without properly preparing for the game's physical demands.

On the field, the ripple effects of poor preparation become evident in the subtle yet critical realm of communication. As an official, your authority is often conveyed through clear, confident directives and explanations. When preparation falters, so too may communication clarity, opening the door to misunderstandings that can quickly escalate tensions among players and coaches.

The consequences of consistent unpreparedness extend beyond the boundaries of a single game, potentially impacting your career. In the close-knit world of sports officiating, reputation is currency. An official known for appearing unprepared may find doors closing and opportunities for prestigious matches slipping away as the professional community's trust wanes. In this way, the penalty for poor preparation is felt in the moment and can echo throughout your officiating journey.

A thorough consideration of your pre-game preparation will help you be organized and, equally important, feel more organized. When you feel organized, your confidence will naturally increase. High-level officiating comes from being as optimally prepared physically, mentally, and logistically as possible.

THE GAME PLAN

Here's how to make pre-game prep your strong suit:

1. *Create your match plan*: Develop a checklist that works for you. Make it personal. This might include reviewing recent rule changes, checking your equipment, or doing light stretching.

2. *Set your targets*: Before each game, pick one or two things you want to achieve. It could be improving your positioning or communicating with assistant referees.

3. *Sharpen your tools*: Keep learning, stay on top of rule changes, and use knowledge to your advantage. Attend workshops, watch game videos, and discuss scenarios with fellow officials.

4. *Build your crew*: Connect with other officials. We're stronger together. Share experiences and tips and support each other's growth.

5. *Know your "why"*: Remind yourself why you do this. It will fuel your fire. Whether you love the sport or desire fair play, keep your motivation front and center.

Your pre-game plan might look something like this:

24 hours before:
- ☐ Lock in game details (double-check time and location)
- ☐ Plan your travel (account for traffic and parking)
- ☐ Lay out your uniform and gear (inspect for any issues)
- ☐ Pack your bag (whistle, cards, watch, notebook, and any sport-specific equipment)

Game day:
- ☐ Fuel up right (balanced meal 2-3 hours before game time)
- ☐ Hydrate consistently (start early and continue throughout the day)

The final countdown:
- ☐ Arrive early (aim for at least 30 minutes before starting)
- ☐ Warm up body and mind (light jog, stretch, and mental rehearsal)
- ☐ Gather with your fellow officials (align on key points and potential challenges)

Remember, this is your show. Tweak this plan until it feels comfortable and natural. The goal? When you step onto the arena, you're not just ready but unstoppable. Your pre-game routine is your foundation for success. Master it, and you'll see the difference in your performance, your confidence, and your enjoyment of the game. Now, go out there and show them what a well-prepared official can do!

RULE 1.2

INSPECT AND PREPARE—THE DEVIL IS IN THE DETAILS

The Call

The need to inspect equipment and the venue makes sense from a logistics perspective. Ensuring you have the equipment you need to officiate and for the competition to proceed will help prevent any unnecessary delays or issues. But have you considered the psychological benefit of doing so? In addition to logistical advantages, conducting thorough inspections can also help reduce worry and boost confidence among officials and participants.

Familiarity with the environment and assurance that all equipment is in proper working order creates a sense of preparedness, allowing everyone to focus more fully on performance. This proactive approach can foster a calm, professional atmosphere, contributing to better decision-making and overall event success.

The Advantage

Being familiar with the venue, its facilities, and background areas won't just save you time by knowing where things are. The focus offers benefits from several psychological perspectives:

☑ *Control and preparedness*: Pre-game inspection and familiarity help to reduce uncertainty and anxiety caused by unknown factors.

☑ *Focus and mindfulness*: The pre-game inspection may be an opportunity to set the tone for your performance mindset. As you inspect the components, you will shift your attention away from distractions and toward the task (and competition).

☑ *Cognitive priming*: Performing a repeated pre-game action related to equipment and venue can help mentally prepare you for the officiating challenges.

☑ *Reinforcement of professional identity*: Checking the venue and inspecting equipment are all part of a referee's authority and responsibility.

☑ *Anxiety reduction*: When inspecting equipment and the venue becomes a regular part of pre-game preparation, the tasks provide a structured and familiar environment for the referee to focus on. This focus can help alleviate any anxiety or worry before a game.

☑ *Environmental comfort*: Inspecting the venue contributes to what some researchers call "environmental comfort." This increased comfort with the surroundings can lead to better spatial awareness during the game, potentially improving positioning and decision-making.

The Penalty

For referees, the mental toll of being disorganized can be particularly heavy. Imagine arriving at the pitch only to realize you've forgotten your whistle or cards or discovering mid-game that you overlooked a crucial equipment check. I once worked with an official who realized, just hours before kickoff, that she'd left the inserts for her boots back at the hotel, tucked inside her training shoes. Fortunately, someone was able to dash across town to retrieve them, but the added stress was the last thing she needed, and the boots only arrived moments before she stepped onto the pitch.

These avoidable oversights disrupt the match's flow and chip away your confidence and focus. The constant worry about what else might go wrong can skyrocket your stress levels, making it harder to make split-second decisions or maintain authority on the field. As the game progresses, you might find yourself second-guessing calls or struggling to keep up with play, all because the consequences of disorganization are draining your mental energy. This can lead to a vicious cycle where each oversight feeds into increased worry, potentially affecting your performance and long-term enjoyment.

The Game Plan

A well-executed pre-game inspection is more than just a checklist—it's essential to setting the tone for a successful officiating performance. By approaching this process with purpose and structure, referees can ensure the playing environment is safe and compliant while mentally preparing themselves for the challenges ahead. Here's an example of how your pre-game inspection routine might look:

1. Arrive at the venue early, allowing ample time for a thorough inspection.
2. Take a deep breath and mentally transition into "referee mode" as you begin the process.
3. Conduct a purposeful walk around the entire playing area.
4. Check all court/field markings, ensuring they are clear and accurate.
5. Inspect goal posts, nets, baskets, or other sport-specific equipment.
6. Examine game balls, verifying proper inflation and condition.
7. If applicable, test any electronic equipment (e.g., communication devices, scoring systems).
8. Incorporate the inspection into a broader pre-match routine, including physical warm-up and mental preparation exercises.

By following these steps, referees can maximize the pre-game inspection routine's practical and psychological benefits. This structured approach helps reduce anxiety, enhance focus, and boost confidence, setting the stage for effective officiating performance.

RULE 1.3

VISUALIZE SUCCESS—MIND OVER MATTER

The Call

Visualization (or mental imagery) is a powerful psychological technique for enhancing performance and decision-making. The human mind constantly thinks and creates scenarios, real or imagined, positive or negative. Visualization is a thinking strategy that helps your brain dial into helpful visual game scenarios and put them into action.

Visualization requires mentally rehearsing scenarios and decisions, which creates and strengthens neural pathways in the brain. Visualizing correct calls or handling challenging situations is programming your mind for success. The more you can see yourself in the right position, making the right call, the more you are priming your body and mind to get into position.

Visualization is effective for sporting referees and officials because mental practice significantly enhances real-world performance.

The Advantage

Visualization can significantly enhance your mental skills and overall officiating performance. By mentally rehearsing game scenarios, you can develop several crucial abilities that directly translate to better decision-making on the field. This practice allows you to train yourself to spot important details faster, recognize common play patterns more easily, and maintain a heightened awareness of multiple elements unfolding simultaneously during a match.

The benefits of visualization extend beyond mere observation skills. Regular mental practice sharpens your ability to focus and anticipate game situations, providing a marked advantage in real-time officiating. Furthermore, visualization is an effective technique for managing pre-game anxiety and building confidence, essential to successful officiating.

One key advantage of this mental training method is its impact on information processing. Referees who consistently practice visualization can process visual information more efficiently and react quickly to events unfolding on the field. This enhanced processing ability allows officials to pick up on relevant cues more effectively and make more informed decisions under the pressure of live game situations.

As referees incorporate visualization into their training regimen, they often find that their nervousness decreases while their preparedness for various game scenarios increases. This mental rehearsal puts you on a path to improved performance, increasing the likelihood of making accurate decisions even in high-pressure moments.

The Penalty

Without effective visualization strategies, officials may involuntarily replay mental images of past errors. This seemingly harmless habit can increase the likelihood of repeating those mistakes and undermine performance. Visualization is a powerful tool for creating success, and without it, referees forgo valuable opportunities to mentally rehearse effective outcomes, improve decision-making skills, and build confidence.

Studies have shown that elite referees make more accurate decisions and exhibit different visual search behaviors than novices. However, by not incorporating visualization into preparation, referees miss out on a crucial strategy for improving their ability to see, understand, and make decisions.

Visualization helps build confidence by mentally practicing success and preparing for tough situations. Without it, you might doubt yourself and hesitate, leading to mistakes when quick decisions are needed. Visualization also helps you better understand the game, improving your awareness and positioning.

Not using visualization means you miss out on important mental training. This can hurt performance and make it harder to handle the challenges of officiating. By skipping this technique, referees are less prepared and may make more mistakes during games.

The Game Plan

Here's a step-by-step guide on how to use visualization as a referee:

Step 1: Create a quiet environment
Find a distraction-free space where you can focus entirely on the visualization exercise. Turn off your phone, close the door, and settle into a comfortable but alert position.

Step 2: Set a clear objective
Decide on specific scenarios you want to visualize. As a referee, you might focus on:
- Calling a penalty in a high-stakes moment
- Managing conflicts between players or coaches
- Positioning yourself for the best view of the action

Step 3: Engage all your senses
Make your visualization multi-sensory for maximum effectiveness:
- Sight: Picture the players, field, and surroundings
- Sound: Imagine the crowd noise, whistle, and player talk
- Touch: Feel the whistle in your hand or the motion of signaling
- Emotion: Envision the calm confidence while making calls

Step 4: Visualize success
Always imagine yourself performing at your best. See yourself:
- Making confident, accurate calls
- Staying composed during difficult interactions
- Positioning yourself perfectly to follow the play

Step 5: Change perspectives
Visualize from different viewpoints:
- First-person perspective (what you would see)
- Third-person perspective (how others would see you)

Step 6: Practice regularly
Dedicate 5-10 minutes to visualization before every game. Make it a routine to enhance your mental readiness gradually.

Step 7: Combine with physical practice
Reinforce your visualization by physically practicing the actions you've mentally rehearsed. For example, practice running the court or field in a real-life setting after visualizing your positioning.

If a visualization turns negative, stop and correct it. By consistently applying these steps, you'll develop sharper focus, quicker reactions, and improved decision-making abilities as a referee.

RULE 1 IN SUMMARY
THE PRE-GAME PLAYBOOK RULE

THINK OF THESE THREE RULES AS PUZZLE PIECES THAT FIT together to get you ready for the game:

Rule 1.1 Preparation: This is your plan. In the same way athletes approach their training, thorough preparation sets up everything else.

Rule 1.2 Inspection: This step turns your plan into action. It helps you focus and enter "referee mode" while ensuring everything is ready.

Rule 1.3 Visualization: This is like practicing in your mind. It uses what you've prepared and what you know about the venue to picture how you'll do well.

Let's think about how these principles could be applied across different sports:

American Football

A high-stakes playoff game at an unfamiliar stadium. Your preparation routine starts 24 hours prior, reviewing team tendencies and recent game films (Rule 1.1). Upon arrival, you methodically inspect the field, paying special attention to the sideline markers and end zone pylons (Rule 1.2). During your final quiet moments, you visualize successfully managing the first snap, hearing the quarterback's cadence, feeling the rhythm of the play clock, and positioning yourself for an optimal view of the line of scrimmage (Rule 1.3).

Gymnastics

Judging a national competition. Your preparation includes reviewing recent rule interpretations and scoring criteria (Rule 1.1). Equipment inspection focuses on checking sight lines from your judging position and lighting conditions (Rule 1.2). Visualization centers on maintaining focus during complex routines and confidently delivering scores under time pressure (Rule 1.3).

Cricket

A multi-day match in challenging conditions. Preparation involves weather forecasts and pitch reports (Rule 1.1). Your inspection routine includes detailed boundary rope checks and light meter readings (Rule 1.2). Visualization focuses on maintaining concentration during long sessions and signaling crucial decisions (Rule 1.3).

In each case, the three principles work together:
- Preparation is your plan
- Inspection is your checklist
- Visualization brings it together

When all three elements align, you create an environment where your confidence flows from thorough preparation, your focus is sharp and clear, your decisions come from a place of readiness, and your authority is built on solid ground.

Remember: Preparation is the silent architect of success.

To implement the learnings from Rule 1 – The Pre-Game Playbook, download your bonus copy of *The Whistle Blower Workbook*.

Scan this QR code or visit: https://books.drjolukins.com/tn2elyoas6

RULE 2

MIND AND BODY IN SYNC

"Every decision starts with a clear mind and a prepared body. That's how you stay sharp under pressure."
—Becky Sauerbrunn

THE IMPORTANCE OF BOTH MENTAL AND PHYSICAL READINESS IN officiating cannot be overstated. Consistent physical preparation and adequate mental rest are essential for enhancing focus, building resilience, and improving overall performance—even when external factors disrupt routines. By prioritizing physical fitness and mental clarity, referees create a strong foundation that enables quick, accurate decisions under pressure and helps them navigate each game with greater confidence and effectiveness.

It's easy to feel tired or overwhelmed with the demands of daily life, which can affect your readiness on game day. By intentionally prioritizing both your physical and mental preparation, you ensure you arrive at each game focused, energized, and ready to perform at your best.

Within Rule 2, we will explore the connection between sleep and fuel and how this affects your mental sharpness when officiating.

Rule 2.1: Sleep Like a Champion—Rest for Success
Rule 2.2: Peak Fitness for Peak Performance—The Physical Edge
Rule 2.3: Fuel Your Mind—Nutrition for Excellence

This next rule emphasizes the critical importance of mind, rest, and fuel for performance. By prioritizing these factors, you lay the foundation to better handle whatever challenges officiating may present.

RULE 2.1

SLEEP LIKE A CHAMPION—REST FOR SUCCESS

The Call

Research in sports such as basketball, tennis, baseball, and cycling has consistently demonstrated that increased sleep leads to improved performance. Whilst more studies are required to better understand it's influence, it is already clear that poor sleep can reduce motivation, physical strength, and decision-making ability. Enhancing sleep quality has been shown to improve reaction times by as much as 17%. Sleep plays a crucial role in the performance and well-being of referees and sporting officials, assisting in physical restoration and enabling optimal thinking.

Sleep serves a vital restorative function for the body and mind. During sleep, particularly in the slow-wave stages, the body repairs tissues regenerates cells and releases human growth hormone. This restoration is essential for physical recovery and maintaining peak cognitive function.

Most people know the importance of sleep, but engage in behaviors that don't allow for the quality or quantity required. It is common for people to stay up later than they intended or to lie in bed, scrolling through their phone when they could be getting valuable minutes of sleep. It's an easy trap to fall into, but more sleep will give you the edge you need.

The Advantage

Quality sleep is critical for the cognitive abilities fundamental to officiating, including attention, decision-making, memory consolidation, and reaction time. Adequate rest enhances your ability to maintain focus, make quick and accurate decisions, retain information, and respond swiftly to changing game situations.

Physical readiness for officiating is also heavily influenced by sleep. Proper rest impacts energy levels, fatigue resistance, coordination, and balance. Importantly, adequate sleep reduces the risk of injury. A study led by Matthew Milewski and colleagues at the Institute for Scholastic Sport Science and Medicine found that young athletes who averaged less than 7 hours of sleep per night faced a 70% higher risk of injury over a 21-month period. This research highlights the crucial role of adequate sleep for well-being and reducing the risk of injury.

Officiating can be highly stressful, and quality sleep is crucial for managing pressure and emotional regulation. Maintaining composure during high-pressure situations is directly linked to the previous night's sleep. Sleep is a restorative process that allows the body to repair and regenerate while consolidating memories and learning from daily experiences.

The consistency of sleep patterns is vital for maintaining the body's natural circadian rhythm, which can be particularly challenging for officials with irregular schedules. By prioritizing sleep, referees and officials can optimize their performance, improve stress management, and ensure long-term health and career longevity.

The Penalty

Sleep deprivation can have profound negative impacts on sporting officials, affecting both their physical and mental performance. Even short periods of insufficient sleep can significantly impair your abilities during competition. In extreme cases, sleep deprivation can cause cognitive impairment comparable to intoxication, leading to compromised decision-making, reduced enjoyment of the role, and overall diminished performance.

Adequate sleep is crucial for injury prevention and overall well-being for officials. While the advice to prioritize sleep may seem straightforward, implementing it often proves challenging, particularly during late hours when the temptation to stay awake is strongest. This is where developing effective nighttime routines becomes essential. By establishing consistent pre-sleep habits, you can make retiring at your optimal bedtime easier and ensure you receive the restorative sleep necessary for peak performance.

The Game Plan

Try this sleep performance challenge to improve sleep quality and quantity. If you prefer, you can keep your notes in your bonus *The Whistle Blower Workbook* (see download link below).

1. Create a sleep log for one week:
- Record bedtime, wake time, and total sleep hours
- Note any disruptions or difficulties falling asleep
- Rate your overall performance the following day (1-10)

   *It's important not to change your usual routine during this week

2. Implement the following sleep performance practices for the next 7 days:
- Establish a consistent bedtime routine in the 30-60 minutes before shutting your eyes in bed
- Avoid screens 90 minutes before bed (that includes phones and tablets)
- Keep your bedroom cool, dark, and quiet

- Limit caffeine and alcohol intake, especially in the evening
3. *Continue the sleep log for another week while following these practices.*
4. *Compare the two weeks:*
- Look for improvements in sleep duration and quality
- Note any changes in your perceived performance ratings
5. *Reflect on which practices had the most significant impact and commit to maintaining them long-term.*

    This activity will help you understand your sleep patterns and the effects of good sleep hygiene on your performance as a referee or official.

For more effective strategies on transforming your sleep habits—or any habits, for that matter—download a free copy of **The Elite Sleep Guide**, which I developed as part of my first book, *The Elite*. This guide features straightforward, practical techniques to help you get a better night's rest.

Scan this QR code or visit: https://books.drjolukins.com/gh859igxsg

RULE 2.2

PEAK FITNESS FOR PEAK PERFORMANCE—
THE PHYSICAL EDGE

The Call

Physical fitness isn't just about keeping up with the game's pace; it's about gaining respect through your presence, making split-second decisions with unwavering confidence, and outlasting the very athletes you officiate. Your body is the cornerstone of your officiating prowess.

Every stride you take, blow of the whistle, and every call you make reflects your physical readiness. Superior fitness allows you to position yourself optimally, reducing the margin for error in your decisions. It sharpens your mental game when fatigue sets in for others, giving you a critical edge in high-stakes moments.

A well-structured pre-match warm-up and post-match recovery routine is crucial for physical and mental preparation in refereeing. Implementing these practices not only primes your body for optimal performance but also serves as a significant confidence booster. The warm-up acts as a mental trigger, signaling to your mind that you're ready to officiate.

The Advantage

In addition to the physical benefits of fitness, being well-conditioned for the court or field offers psychological benefits. Officiating demands psychological resilience to handle pressure, abuse, and high-stakes decision-making. Regular physical training enhances mental toughness, helping you maintain composure in challenging situations.

A well-conditioned body is your armor against injury and your ticket to longevity in the demands of officiating. Recovery occurs faster, allowing you to perform at your best game after game, season after season. Remember, your physical presence sets the tone for the game.

A thorough warm-up increases blood flow, raises body temperature, and prepares muscles and joints for the demands of the game. This physical preparation can significantly reduce the risk of injuries during the match. Warming up provides further benefit by helping to focus the mind, reducing pre-match anxiety and enhancing concentration. This mental readiness is crucial for making quick, accurate decisions on the field.

Knowing you've taken extra steps to prepare your body can provide a psychological edge, similar to the confidence gained from making a correct call during the match. This boost in self-assurance can positively impact your performance throughout the game. Additionally, a structured post-match routine aids in faster recovery, reducing muscle soreness and fatigue, which is particularly important for referees with multiple assignments in close succession.

By prioritizing your physical and mental fitness, you ensure you're in the best possible position to make fair judgments, maintain control of the game, and preserve your passion for officiating. Remember, a fit referee contributes to a more equitable, more enjoyable sporting experience for everyone involved.

The Penalty

Physical demands can be intense. Referees in soccer cover 6-8 miles per match, rivaling midfield players, while basketball officials sprint repeatedly up and down the court. On average, boundary referees in the Australian Football League run just under 10 miles per game, with a third of those backwards! You'll struggle to keep up with play without proper conditioning, leading to poor positioning and missed calls.

Mental sharpness declines as physical exhaustion sets in, and fatigue impairs decision-making. This affects your ability to make split-second judgments, especially in the crucial final minutes of a game. Research led by Gary McEwan and colleagues (2024) has shown that soccer referees with higher fitness levels are better able to maintain decision-making accuracy throughout matches, while those experiencing greater physical strain are significantly more likely to make errors as fatigue sets in.

Poor physical condition makes you more susceptible to overuse injuries like shin splints and muscle strains. This can sideline you for extended periods, potentially jeopardizing your officiating career. Players, coaches, and spectators respect officials who demonstrate the same physical commitment expected from athletes. Appearing out of shape undermines your authority on the field.

The Game Plan

Your physical training requires careful and professional attention. Whilst beyond the scope of this book to design your physical fitness regime, it certainly is something I would highly recommend. If you need assistance, I recommend seeking a qualified professional. You may consider a certified personal trainer (CPT), exercise physiologist, athletic trainer, strength and conditioning coach, group fitness instructor, sports performance coach, functional movement specialist, biomechanist or physical therapist.

Here are some questions you could ask yourself to address issues around your physical training:

☐ Am I consistently meeting my fitness goals for each training session?

☐ How well am I recovering between matches and training sessions?

☐ Are there any areas of physical fitness where I'm falling short of the demands of my matches?

☐ How effectively am I balancing my physical training, officiating schedule, and other life commitments?

☐ Am I incorporating enough variety in my workouts to prevent boredom and plateaus?

☐ How does my current fitness level compare to the standards required for my level of officiating?

☐ Are there any recurring injuries or physical issues that I need to address in my training?

☐ Are there any new training techniques or technologies that could benefit my physical preparation?

☐ How well am I tracking and measuring my progress in physical fitness?

RULE 2.3

FUEL YOUR MIND—NUTRITION FOR EXCELLENCE

THE CALL

Your body is not just a physical instrument; it's a complex machine that requires the right fuel to operate at its peak. Proper nutrition is the foundation for mental toughness and officiating excellence. It's not just about eating, it's about strategically nourishing your body and mind to meet the demands of your role.

Every decision you make, every sprint to keep up with play, and every moment of intense focus draws upon the energy reserves you've built through proper nutrition. A well-fueled body supports clear thinking, enhances alertness, and provides the stamina needed to maintain composure under pressure.

Your secret weapon against fatigue and mental fog is a consistent and balanced approach to your nutrition. It allows you to stay sharp when others are flagging, giving you the mental edge in the crucial final moments of a match. Remember, your nutritional choices set the stage for your performance long before you step onto the field.

In mental toughness, proper nutrition is the silent partner to your physical preparation. It's the unseen foundation that supports every aspect of your officiating. A referee who prioritizes nutrition doesn't just show up to the game—they arrive ready to excel from the first whistle to the last.

The Advantage

Proper nutrition has further psychological benefits that extend far beyond the physical. A well-nourished body fosters a resilient mind, which is crucial for the mental demands of officiating. Here's how balanced nutrition bolsters your mental toughness:

☑ Supports brain health, improving your decision-making abilities and reaction times.

☑ Helps regulate mood, allowing you to maintain composure in high-pressure situations.

☑ Knowing you're properly fueled boosts your self-assurance on the field.

☑ Helps your body better cope with the physical and mental stresses of officiating.

☑ Prevents energy crashes, helping you maintain focus throughout the match.

By prioritizing nutrition alongside your physical training, you're equipping yourself with a powerful tool for mental resilience. Remember, a well-nourished referee is better prepared to handle the psychological challenges of officiating, contributing to fairer games and a more rewarding experience for all involved.

The Penalty

Referees who neglect proper nutrition risk more than just physical fatigue. Poor dietary habits can significantly impact mental performance, affecting your decision making. Inadequate nutrition is linked to increased risks of depression, anxiety, and mood disorders, compromising your emotional stability on the field. Cognitive functions crucial for refereeing—like decision-making, focus, and memory—can deteriorate, leading to missed calls and poor game management. Further, nutritional deficiencies can lower your stress resilience, making it harder to handle the pressures of officiating. By prioritizing a balanced diet rich in essential nutrients, you're not just fueling your body, you're sharpening your mind. Remember, mental toughness starts with what's on your plate, so fuel yourself for success.

The Game Plan

While proper nutrition is crucial for a referee's performance, providing specific dietary advice is beyond the scope of this book. However, I strongly recommend seeking professional guidance to optimize your nutritional intake. Consider consulting a registered dietitian (RD), sports nutritionist, certified nutrition specialist (CNS), or a physician specializing in nutrition.

To help you reflect on your current nutritional habits and their impact on your officiating performance, consider the following questions:

- ☐ Am I consistently fueling my body with balanced meals before and after matches?
- ☐ How does my energy level fluctuate throughout a match, and could it be related to my nutrition?
- ☐ Am I staying adequately hydrated before, during, and after officiating?
- ☐ Do I notice any changes in my focus or decision-making abilities based on what I've eaten?
- ☐ How well am I balancing my nutritional needs with my officiating schedule and lifestyle?
- ☐ Are there any specific foods that affect my performance positively or negatively?
- ☐ Am I consuming enough nutrients to support my recovery between matches and training sessions?

☐ How does my current diet align with the nutritional recommendations for high-performance officials?
☐ Should I consider incorporating any new nutritional strategies or supplements?
☐ How well am I planning my meals to ensure optimal nutrition, especially on match days?

Reflecting on these questions can help you identify areas for improvement in your nutrition strategy, ultimately supporting your mental and physical performance on the field.

RULE 2 IN SUMMARY
THE MIND AND BODY IN SYNC RULE

THINK OF THESE THREE PRINCIPLES AS PUZZLE PIECES THAT FIT together to create your physical and mental foundation for peak performance:
Rule 2.1 Sleep: Forms your recovery base. Like recharging a battery, quality sleep restores both body and mind.
Rule 2.2 Physical fitness: Provides your performance platform. When your body is well-conditioned, your mind follows suit.
Rule 2.3 Nutrition: Fuels both systems. Proper fueling maintains mental clarity and emotional stability.

Let's consider how these principles could be applied across different sports:
Rugby Union
    It is late in the second half of a high-intensity match. Quality sleep means your decision-making remains sharp despite fatigue (Rule 2.1). Your fitness base allows you to maintain perfect positioning for scrums (Rule 2.2). Proper nutrition stabilizes your energy

levels, allowing you to manage a heated forward battle with calm authority (Rule 2.3).

Cricket

Officiating an all-day or multi-day competition requires sustained mental focus. Your sleep routine ensures cognitive clarity through multiple sessions (Rule 2.1). Physical fitness helps maintain proper posture and alertness during long observation periods (Rule 2.2). Strategic nutrition timing maintains steady blood sugar for consistent accuracy (Rule 2.3).

Athletics

Managing a full day of track events demands sustained energy. Quality sleep ensures quick reaction times for false starts (Rule 2.1). Your fitness allows quick movements between positions (Rule 2.2). Proper nutrition maintains concentration through changing weather and long delays (Rule 2.3).

In each case, the three principles work together:
- Sleep is your restoration
- Fitness is your capability
- Nutrition is your fuel

RULE 2 IN SUMMARY   41

When all three elements align, you create an environment where your decisions stay sharp under pressure, your presence commands respect, your energy sustains through overtime and your confidence flows from the preparation.

Remember: Your body and mind are one system—neglect either and both suffer.

To implement the learnings from Rule 2 – Mind and Body in Sync, download your bonus copy of *The Whistle Blower Workbook*.

Scan this QR code or visit: https://books.drjolukins.com/tn2elyoas6

RULE 3

MASTER YOUR TIME

"Anticipate the future and adapt accordingly."
—Wayne Gretzky

IMAGINE YOU ARE IN THE MIDDLE OF A CRUCIAL MATCH, whistle in hand when suddenly your mind drifts to that controversial call you made last week. In that split second of distraction, you miss a key offside. Has that ever happened to you? Referees often highlight how their time focus or time attention affects their performance.

What is time attention? It's essentially what *time zone* your mind is focused on: the past, present, or future. Staying present in the moment and using past experiences to prepare for what's ahead is the simple but challenging requirement of good officiating. While it's natural for our minds to wander between the past, present, and future, the best refs know how to keep their focus where it needs to be.

Under Rule 3, we will explore how understanding and managing your sense of time can fundamentally impact officiating performance.

Rule 3.1: Arrive Early, Leave Later—The Time Advantage
Rule 3.2: Learn from the Past, Stay in the Present, Be Ready for the Future—Timeless Wisdom
Rule 3.3: Plan for Overtime Before It Happens—Anticipate and Adapt

This rule is all about using time to your advantage. By learning from what's happened previously, staying focused on what's happening now, and being ready for what might happen next, you'll make better calls and handle games more smoothly. It's about being in the right headspace at the right time, from the pre-game preparations to the final whistle.

RULE 3.1

ARRIVE EARLY, LEAVE LATER—THE TIME ADVANTAGE

The Call

As a referee, arriving early for a game is more than just good timing—it's a behavior with significant psychological benefits. Sometimes, officials struggle with punctuality not out of disrespect but due to challenges in accurately estimating preparation time or getting waylaid in other tasks. Interestingly, when people plan for the future, there is an observable human phenomenon of anticipating that we will have more time at our disposal and that tasks will take less time than they do. It's not your fault; it's a natural human bias! Having strategies to avoid this is important, and developing the mental tools to prioritize early arrival is crucial for peak performance.

The Advantage

Arriving early and staying back later after a game offers numerous benefits that can significantly enhance your officiating performance. This practice contributes to enhanced mental preparation, allowing you to reduce pre-game worry and stress by eliminating the need to rush. The extra time provides an opportunity to boost your self-confidence through thorough preparation, improve your mental focus, and get yourself truly ready for the match. Being more organised offers valuable moments for visualization and mental rehearsal of various game scenarios, setting you up for success.

This approach also fosters professionalism. By consistently arriving early and staying late, you demonstrate reliability and respect for the game, qualities highly valued in officiating. These extra moments create opportunities to build rapport with players and coaches, enhancing your ability to manage the game effectively. You'll also have the time to deal with any unexpected issues that may arise and review rules or strategies specific to the match at hand. Perhaps most importantly, this practice optimizes your performance on the field or court. It allows for a proper physical and mental warm-up, ensuring you're at your best when the game begins. You'll have time to familiarize yourself with the environment and conditions, reducing the risk of early-game errors that can occur when you're rushed. This thorough preparation enhances your ability to start the match with authority, setting a positive tone for officiating throughout the game.

Post-match, staying later may allow you to debrief with your referee colleagues and mentors, warm down, and perform any helpful physical recovery after the game. By embracing arriving early and staying late, you're not just managing time, you're leveraging it to become a more effective, confident, and respected official.

The Penalty

Frequently arriving just in time and leaving immediately after the final whistle can have significant downsides in your officiating career. This rushed approach often results in compromised decision-making. The increased stress and anxiety from cutting it close can negatively affect your judgment, while the lack of proper preparation time may impact your ability to make critical calls accurately. Being in a hurried state limits your ability to adapt to unexpected situations or changes, increasing the risk of errors or oversights that could have been avoided with better time management.

Such behavior can also damage your professional reputation. Consistently arriving late or leaving immediately after games may create a perception of disorganization or unprofessionalism. You miss out on valuable pre- and post-game interactions that could enhance your understanding of the game and build important relationships. Over time, this approach could lead to the loss of high-profile assignments or advancement opportunities, as reliability and thoroughness are highly valued in officiating circles.

The negative psychological impact of this habit shouldn't be underestimated, either. Chronic stress from constant rushing can damage your mental health, reducing your enjoyment and engagement in officiating. You may develop what's often called "hurry sickness," a constant urgency that can affect your overall well-being. Additionally, rushing away after each match makes you miss crucial opportunities for reflection and learning, hindering your growth as an official.

By consistently arriving early and staying late, referees create a buffer for better preparation, reduced stress, and enhanced overall performance. It's an investment in your officiating career that pays dividends in improved performance, professional growth, and personal satisfaction.

The Game Plan

To help yourself be ahead of time, I would recommend you work backward and overestimate how long things will take you; if you think it will take 3 minutes to grab your bag, shoes, and water bottle (don't forget to fill it!), and a recovery snack, then allow 7 minutes. Working backward can look like this to ensure you arrive at the stadium by 6:00 PM:

Night before game:

Pack referee bag with essential equipment (whistle, cards, watch, flags, etc.) (10 minutes)

Check and prepare uniform (clean shirt, shorts, socks, and shoes) (15 minutes)

Ensure all electronic devices (phone, watch) are fully charged (5 minutes)

Review match details (teams, venue, kickoff time, competition rules) (5 minutes)

Day of game:

4:25 PM - Study recent rule changes or interpretations (10 minutes)

4:35 PM - Mentally rehearse game scenarios and decision-making processes (10 minutes)

4:45 PM - Perform light stretching or warm-up exercises (15 minutes)

5:00 PM - Eat a light, nutritious pre-game meal (20 minutes)

5:20 PM - Check the weather forecast and ensure appropriate gear if needed (5 minutes)

5:25 PM - Ensure all electronic devices (phone, watch) are fully charged (5 minutes)

5:30 PM - Plan travel route and check for potential traffic delays (10 minutes)

5:40 PM - Leave home for the stadium (20-minute drive)

6:00 PM - Arrive at the stadium

This schedule allows you to complete all necessary preparations and arrive at the stadium by 6:00 PM. The total preparation time is 1 hour and 35 minutes, starting at 4:25 PM. This timeline provides a structured approach to ensure you are fully prepared and punctual for the game.

RULE 3.2

LEARN FROM THE PAST, STAY IN THE PRESENT, BE READY FOR THE FUTURE— TIMELESS WISDOM

THE CALL

Our brains can navigate through time, effortlessly shifting between past experiences, the present moment, and future anticipation. This mental flexibility is particularly valuable for referees, who must draw upon their past experiences, maintain focus in the present, and prepare for future scenarios. The ability to mentally time travel allows you to make informed decisions, stay alert to current game dynamics, and anticipate potential challenges.

This mental agility is not just a useful skill, it's a fundamental aspect of human thinking that plays a crucial role in our decision-making processes. For referees, it becomes an indispensable tool in your officiating arsenal. By tapping into past experiences, you can quickly recall similar situations and the outcomes of your previous decisions, informing current judgments. Simultaneously, maintaining a sharp focus on the present allows you to react swiftly and accurately to the ever-changing dynamics as the game unfolds.

The ability to project into the future is equally important. It enables referees to anticipate potential scenarios, prepare for various outcomes, and confidently make split-second decisions. This forward-thinking approach also helps manage the game's overall flow and tempo, ensuring fair play and adherence to rules. How might this look for you as a referee? Let's consider this in two sports—football and volleyball.

Football
Past: As I step onto the pitch for today's match, I recall my last game, a heated derby between rival clubs. The atmosphere was electric, with fans packed into the stadium. I had to make several crucial decisions, including a controversial penalty call that ultimately decided the match. The experience taught me the importance of maintaining composure under pressure.
Present: Now, I stand at the center circle, whistle in hand, ready to kick off today's game. The teams are lined up, waiting for my signal. I take a deep breath, focusing on the task at hand. My mind is clear, alert, and ready to make split-second decisions. I remind myself to stay sharp, keep up with the play, and communicate effectively with my assistants.
Future: Next week, I'll be officiating a crucial playoff match. I visualize myself preparing in the locker room, going through my pre-game routine. I imagine the game's intensity, the crowd's roar, and the responsibility on my shoulders. I mentally rehearse potential scenarios, building my confidence for any situation that may arise.

Volleyball
Past: My last match was a nail-biting five-setter between two evenly matched teams. I remember the challenge of maintaining focus throughout the lengthy contest, especially during the tense final set. The experience reinforced the importance of consistent decision-making and clear signaling throughout a match.
Present: As I stand at the official's platform, I survey the court before me. The teams are warming up, and there's a buzz of anticipation in the air. I run through my mental checklist: net height, court lines, ball

pressure. My mind is focused on the present moment, ready to officiate this match with precision and fairness.

Future: In two days, I'll be refereeing a national championship match. I picture myself arriving at the venue, feeling the weight of the occasion. I envision the dynamic rallies, the need for quick and accurate calls, and the importance of maintaining a calm demeanor. I mentally prepare for the challenges that high-stakes matches often bring.

This mental time travel exercise demonstrates the importance of learning from past experiences, staying focused on the present moment, and preparing for future challenges. You can enhance your performance and decision-making abilities on the field or court by consciously directing your thoughts.

Remember, a successful referee can draw on experience, remain present in the moment, and anticipate potential scenarios, all while maintaining composure and fairness throughout the match. Your challenge as a referee is to have your head in the right place at the right time.

The Advantage

The key advantage of brain flexibility is its impact to enhance a referee's adaptability. Sports events are unpredictable, and officials must be ready to handle unexpected situations. By constantly shifting between past lessons, present observations, and future possibilities, referees can adapt their approach in real time, maintaining control and fairness throughout the match.

Developing and honing this cognitive skill is critical to referee training and development. It goes beyond merely memorizing rules or perfecting hand signals; it's about cultivating a mindset that can seamlessly integrate lessons from the past, awareness of the present, and preparation for the future. This holistic approach to officiating improves the quality of decision-making and contributes to the overall integrity and enjoyment of the sport.

The ability to consciously direct your thoughts to the appropriate time frame is essential for peak performance as an official. It allows you to:

- Make accurate, real-time decisions during games.
- Learn from past experiences without dwelling on them.
- Prepare for future events without becoming overwhelmed by anticipation.
- Maintain focus and composure in high-pressure situations.
- Achieve better work-life balance by being present in off-field activities.

The Penalty

Directing your focus to the appropriate time perspective is a crucial psychological skill for officials. Getting mentally trapped in the wrong moment can misdirect and overload your thinking, increasing the risk of poor decisions.

Consider the following scenario: A coach challenges a decision you have made. Two minutes later, a critical play unfolds, demanding an immediate decision on who hit the ball out of bounds. In this crucial moment, your focus is trapped in the previous challenge when it should be fully on the present. This misalignment can lead to missed calls or incorrect decisions, potentially impacting the game's outcome.

This skill extends beyond the realm of sports officiating. Picture yourself at 2am, wide awake while the world slumbers. Your thoughts race towards the announcement of finals allocations, fluctuating between excitement and anxiety about your potential assignment. In this instance, your mind is unhelpfully projected into the future, preventing you from experiencing restful sleep that can only occur in the present moment.

The Game Plan

My book *Belief: Building Unshakeable Confidence*, illustrates the interplay between past, present, and future in our thinking processes. The image that follows shows an individual navigating through the three temporal dimensions, highlighting the complex nature of our thought patterns and decision-making processes.

Keep your head in the *right* place at the *right* time

For officials, the ability to consciously direct focus to the appropriate temporal perspective is crucial. The key to peak performance lies in mental agility:
- Being fully engaged in the present when making critical calls.
- Reflecting thoughtfully when analyzing past performances.
- Thinking ahead when preparing for future challenges.

This mental flexibility is essential for maintaining top form on and off the field or court.

The foundation for developing this skill is awareness, the ability to dial into your current thought focus. Practice identifying whether your thoughts are directed towards the past, future, or present moment. Once mindful, evaluate if this focus is the most beneficial for the current situation. If not, a shift may be necessary.

Referees often need assistance redirecting their thoughts from the past or future to the present. A simple yet effective three-step process can help:

1. *Take a breath*: Mental strategies are more effective when you're relaxed in the moment.
2. *Anchor yourself*: Focus on something in your immediate environment (use your senses – what can you see, hear or feel?)
3. *Redirect attention*: As you become aware of the present moment, consciously focus on the task.

This strategy is particularly useful during sleepless nights. Cycle yourself through what you can see, hear, and feel, momentarily stopping each sentence. This simple practice can help quiet a racing mind and induce sleep.

By mastering this skill of temporal focus, referees can enhance their decision-making abilities, maintain composure under pressure, and improve overall performance in their officiating duties.

RULE 3.3

PLAN FOR OVERTIME BEFORE IT HAPPENS—ANTICIPATE AND ADAPT

The Call

Overtime situations are high-pressure moments that test a referee's mental fortitude. To maintain composure and make accurate decisions during these critical periods, officials must prepare well in advance. This mental rule emphasizes the importance of proactive planning for overtime scenarios. In such moments, referees face amplified scrutiny from players, coaches, and fans, and every call can significantly impact the outcome of the game. Developing mental toughness through techniques like controlled breathing, positive self-talk, and staying present helps officials remain decisive and resilient, ensuring they uphold fairness and integrity even when emotions run high.

The Advantage

Planning for overtime before it occurs offers referees a significant edge in managing extended play scenarios. This proactive approach helps reduce anxiety and uncertainty when faced with the prospect of additional periods. By mentally preparing for overtime situations, officials can make more confident and accurate decisions under the increased pressure that often accompanies these crucial game moments.

Anticipating overtime also allows referees to better maintain their focus and energy throughout the additional period. They can mentally prepare strategies to stay sharp and alert, even as fatigue sets in for both players and officials. By being prepared, this forethought enables referees to anticipate potential challenges that might arise during overtime and prepare appropriate responses in advance.

Perhaps most importantly, planning for overtime ensures consistent application of overtime rules and procedures. Referees who have reviewed and internalized these specific regulations are less likely to make errors or hesitate when implementing them in the heat of the moment.

Consider, for instance, a well-prepared basketball referee handling a double overtime situation. Having anticipated this possibility, they would confidently manage the extended play, knowing exactly how many timeouts each team has left and smoothly transitioning between periods without confusion. This level of preparedness not only enhances the referee's performance but also contributes to a fair and well-managed game, regardless of how long it lasts.

The Penalty

Failing to plan for overtime can have serious consequences for officials, potentially compromising their performance during these critical moments of a game. When referees are caught off-guard by extended play, they often experience increased stress and mental fatigue, precisely when clear thinking and decisive action are most needed.

This lack of preparation can lead to inconsistent or incorrect application of overtime rules, as officials may struggle to recall specific regulations under pressure. Consequently, their confidence in decision-making may waver, affecting the authority and control they maintain over the game. Overtime increases the intensity, pressure, and expectations for players, coaches, and spectators. Unprepared referees might find it challenging to manage the expectations of others and themselves during overtime, potentially escalating game tensions. Perhaps most concerning is the increased risk of errors that could significantly impact the game's outcome. These mistakes, made in high-stakes moments, can have far-reaching consequences for teams and players.

Imagine, for example, a soccer referee who finds themselves unprepared for a penalty shootout. They might struggle to remember the correct order of kicks or fail to track which players have already taken their shots properly. Such oversights could lead to a disputed outcome, tarnishing the integrity of the match and potentially affecting league standings or tournament progressions.

By failing to anticipate and prepare for overtime scenarios, referees not only put themselves at a disadvantage but also risk compromising the fairness and smooth execution of the game they're entrusted to oversee.

The Game Plan

To effectively plan for overtime, referees should:

1. Study and internalize overtime rules:

- Thoroughly review the specific overtime regulations for your sport and league.
- Understand any differences between regular season and playoff overtime procedure.
- Practice visualizing various overtime scenarios and your responses to them.

An ice hockey referee might review the NHL's 3-on-3 overtime format and shootout procedures, ensuring they're prepared for both regular season and playoff scenarios.

2. *Develop a mental checklist*:
- Create a brief mental list of key points to review before overtime begins.
- Include items such as timeouts remaining, player eligibility, and any specific overtime rules.

A football referee could create a checklist that includes verifying the number of timeouts each team has, confirming sudden death rules, and reviewing overtime coin toss procedures.

3. *Establish clear communication protocols*:
- Discuss overtime procedures with your officiating crew before the game.
- Agree on how you'll communicate important information during overtime.
- Plan how to convey overtime rules to team captains and coaches effectively.

A volleyball officiating team might agree on specific hand signals to use during a fifth-set tiebreaker to quickly communicate serve order or rotation errors.

4. *Prepare physically and mentally*:
- Incorporate endurance training into your routine to maintain stamina during extended play.
- Practice relaxation techniques to manage stress during high-pressure moments.
- Use visualization to rehearse successful overtime officiating mentally.

A baseball umpire could incorporate high-intensity interval training to improve endurance for extra innings and practice deep breathing exercises to stay calm during tense moments.

5. Review past experiences:
- Reflect on previous overtime situations you've officiated.
- Identify areas for improvement and successful strategies to replicate.
- Discuss overtime experiences with fellow officials to gain additional insights.

An ice hockey referee might recall a previous overtime game where they struggled to manage a coach's behavior and develop strategies to improve communication and control in future situations.

6. Stay updated on rule changes:
- Regularly check for any updates or modifications to overtime rules.
- Attend officiating clinics or workshops that cover overtime procedures.
- Participate in online forums or discussions about overtime officiating challenges.

A tennis umpire could attend an annual rules clinic that covers changes to tiebreak procedures in Grand Slam tournaments, ensuring they're prepared for any format adjustments.

By implementing these strategies, referees can approach overtime situations with confidence, clarity, and composure. The key to successful overtime officiating lies in thorough preparation. By investing time and effort into planning for these high-stakes situations, referees can significantly enhance their performance when it matters most, ultimately contributing to a fair and well-managed conclusion to closely contested games.

RULE 3 IN SUMMARY
THE MASTER YOUR TIME RULE

THINK OF THESE THREE PRINCIPLES AS PUZZLE PIECES THAT FIT together to enhance your performance as a referee through effective time management:

Rule 3.1. Avoiding the rush: By always arriving early and leaving later, you allow time to prepare and focus.

Rule 3.2. Time orientation: Keeping your head in the right place at the right time helps you perform at your peak.

Rule 3.3. Anticipation: Preparing for overtime before it happens helps you manage high pressure situations with clarity and confidence.

Let's think about how these principles could be applied across different sports:

American Football

An NFL referee arrives at the stadium hours before kickoff, allowing time to inspect the field, meet with the officiating crew, and mentally prepare (Rule 3.1). During the game, they draw on past experiences to make quick decisions, while staying focused on current play (Rule 3.2). As the game progresses, they anticipate potential scenarios like overtime and how this could play out (Rule 3.3).

Basketball

An NBA official arrives at the arena well before tip-off, reviewing rules and discussing strategies with fellow officials. (Rule 3.1). Throughout the game, they apply lessons from previous matches, while maintaining a sharp focus on current play (Rule 3.2). During time-out breaks, they mentally prepare for possible last-second shot situations (Rule 3.3).

Baseball

An MLB umpire arrives at the ballpark early to check field conditions and review lineups (Rule 3.1). During the game, they recall past rulings to ensure consistency, switching back to the present seamlessly, staying alert to every pitch, (Rule 3.2.). While resting during innings breaks, they anticipate potential extra-inning situations (Rule 3.3).

In each case, the three principles work together:
- Avoiding the rush enhances professionalism
- Time orientation sharpens your focus
- Anticipation sets you up for success

When all three elements align, you create an environment where you project confidence and professionalism, your decision-making is more accurate and consistent, and you're better equipped to handle unexpected situations.

RULE 3 IN SUMMARY

Remember: Excellence in officiating begins long before the opening whistle and extends beyond the final one.

To implement the learnings from Rule 3 – Master your Time, download your bonus copy of *The Whistle Blower Workbook*.

Scan this QR code or visit: https://books.drjolukins.com/tn2elyoas6

PART 2

THE MENTAL PILLARS OF PERFORMANCE

OFFICIATING IN SPORTS IS A COMPLEX AND CHALLENGING ROLE that requires a unique set of skills and a deep understanding of the game. As an official, you are tasked with maintaining order, ensuring fair play, and upholding the integrity of the sport.

Within Part II, we consider the three fundamental pillars that form the backbone of effective officiating, each designed to enhance your performance and contribute to a positive sporting experience for all involved:

Rule 4: The Power of the Whistle

Learn how to wield your whistle with authority, making impactful decisions that shape the course of the game.

Rule 5: Split-Second Clarity

To help you make crystal-clear decisions in the blink of an eye, even when the pressure is at its peak, maintaining the smooth flow of the game.

Rule 6: Command, Connect, and Focus

Discover strategies to inspire respect, foster understanding, and maintain focus through effective communication strategies.

This section will explore the crucial elements that keep your mind focused: control, clarity, and communication. These components are essential in building your mental toughness and enhancing your effectiveness on the field or court. In officiating, mental strength isn't just an asset—it's the foundation upon which excellence is built.

By mastering these fundamental rules, you'll be well-equipped to handle the challenges of officiating with professionalism and skill.

Remember: Effective officiating is not just about enforcing rules; it's about facilitating fair and enjoyable competition through control, clarity, and communication.

RULE 4

THE POWER OF THE WHISTLE

"You can't always control circumstances. However, you can always control your attitude, approach, and response."
—Tony Dungy

CONVERSATIONS WITH REFEREES OFTEN HIGHLIGHT HOW feeling in control boosts their confidence when officiating. Two key elements stand out: knowing what you can and can't control and using your authority wisely. While we can't control everything in a game, understanding how to use our influence makes a big difference.

Feeling in control is about recognizing how your mindset and reactions shape the flow of the game. When referees stay grounded and respond thoughtfully rather than react impulsively, they reinforce their authority and set clear expectations for players and coaches. This ability to manage emotions and maintain composure, even in high-pressure moments, not only supports fair decision-making but also fosters respect from everyone on the court.

In Rule 4, we'll explore how control affects your officiating through three key rules:

Rule 4.1: Control What You Can, Accept What You Can't—The Art of Letting Go
Rule 4.2: Think Before You Act—Consequences of Each Call
Rule 4.3: Influence Through Presence—Your Body Speaks First

Effective officiating isn't about being the loudest or using your whistle most frequently. It's about maintaining game flow through your presence alone.

By mastering these principles, you'll enhance your control on the field, make better decisions under pressure, and maintain the game's integrity with confidence and authority.

RULE 4.1

CONTROL WHAT YOU CAN, ACCEPT WHAT YOU CAN'T—THE ART OF LETTING GO

THE CALL

As a referee or umpire, you're no stranger to the unpredictable nature of sports. One moment, you're overseeing a routine play, and the next, you're at the center of a controversial call that could change the course of the game. It's in these moments that the desire for control can be overwhelming, yet ironically, it's when you have the least control over external factors!

Think about those times when you've made a call, only to have players, coaches, and spectators erupt in disagreement. Or consider instances when weather conditions suddenly change, forcing you to make quick decisions about player safety and game continuity. These scenarios highlight the two key frustrations many officials face: the challenge of maintaining composure when events feel chaotic and unpredictable, and the strong desire to be in control of every aspect of the game.

The Advantage

When you master the art of appropriately focusing on what you can control and investing less of your time in the elements you can't, you will have more mental space to think about the elements where you can actually make a difference. This flexibility in your thinking can feel quite "freeing" and takes far less emotional energy than continually being frustrated by things you cannot influence.

The benefits of mastering this principle include:

- ☑ *Enhanced well-being and lower anxiety*: By focusing on controllable factors, you reduce mental stress and emotional turbulence, leading to a more balanced state of mind.
- ☑ *A greater sense of personal power*: Shifting your mindset from passive to proactive enhances your feeling of agency and control over your performance.
- ☑ *Improved productivity and goal achievement*: Concentrating on actionable goals within your control creates a positive feedback loop, boosting motivation and performance.
- ☑ *Strengthened emotional resilience*: Managing your reactions to controllable factors helps you maintain composure and clarity, especially in high-pressure situations.
- ☑ *Better relationships with others*: By controlling your responses to what truly matters, you improve your ability to handle conflicts and collaborate effectively with players, coaches, and fellow officials.
- *Release from unnecessary stress*: Accepting the limits of your control eliminates the exhaustion that comes from trying to influence external outcomes beyond your reach.

Additionally, this principle fosters a performance mindset. By focusing on elements within your control, such as your preparation, positioning, and decision-making process, you create opportunities for continuous improvement. This approach allows you to view challenges as learning experiences rather than insurmountable obstacles, contributing to long-term professional development and satisfaction in your role as an official.

The Penalty

Failing to master how to control the controllables can have significant consequences for an official's performance, outcome, and general well-being. When uncontrollable factors take too much of your attention, it may make it difficult for you to maintain focus on crucial elements of the game, such as positioning or player behavior. This can lead to missed calls or poor judgment, especially when combined with physical fatigue and general game stress.

The inability to distinguish between controllable and uncontrollable factors can lead to an avalanche of negative outcomes. Officials may experience increased self-doubt and second-guessing, which can erode confidence and decision-making abilities over time. This hesitation can be perceived by players and coaches, potentially undermining your authority on the field or court.

The stress of trying to control uncontrollable elements can also have a physical impact, leading to tension, fatigue, and decreased reaction times. This physical toll can significantly affect your ability to keep up with the pace of the game, especially in crucial moments when peak performance is essential.

Furthermore, constantly worrying about factors beyond your control can create a negative mindset, making you more susceptible to criticism and less resilient in the face of challenges. This can lead to a self-fulfilling prophecy where your fears of losing control actually contribute to a loss of control in your officiating.

The Game Plan

To overcome this challenge, focus on factors within your control while being aware of the level of influence you have over each element. Stephen Covey's "Circle of Influence Framework" provides a powerful tool for referees to navigate the complex landscape of officiating. This model categorizes factors into three concentric circles: the Circle of Control (innermost), the Circle of Influence (middle), and the Circle of Concern (outermost).

1. *Identify your circles*: Clearly define what falls into each circle for your officiating role.
- In your Circle of Control, include elements like your preparation, fitness level, knowledge of rules, and in-game decisions.
- Your Circle of Influence might contain factors like communication with players and coaches, game tempo, and positioning.
- The Circle of Concern encompasses elements like weather conditions, spectator behavior, or league policies.

2. *Develop a pre-game routine*: Create a consistent pre-game routine focusing on controllable factors. This might include:
- A thorough equipment check.
- A specific warm-up sequence to ensure physical readiness.
- A mental preparation ritual, such as visualization or breathing exercises.
- A brief review of key rules or points of emphasis for the game.
(For reminders on how to develop this further, refer to Rule 1.1.)

3. *Implement in-game strategies*: During the game, use techniques to maintain focus on controllable elements:
- Use a trigger word or physical gesture to reset your focus when distracted by the uncontrollable.

- Practice mindfulness techniques to stay present and aware of your immediate surroundings.
- Develop a consistent decision-making process to rely on in high-pressure moments.

4. *Utilize natural breaks*: Use timeouts, quarter breaks, or other natural pauses in play to reassess and refocus on your circles of control and influence. This might involve:
- A quick body scan to check for tension and release it.
- A brief mental review of your performance so far, focusing on areas you can improve.
- Setting a specific intention for the next period of play.

5. *Post-game reflection*: After each game, engage in structured reflection:
- Identify situations where you successfully focused on controllable factors.
- Recognize moments where uncontrollable elements distracted you.
- Develop specific strategies to improve your focus for future games.

By consistently applying these strategies, you'll develop a more nuanced understanding of what you can and cannot control. This awareness will allow you to channel your energy more effectively, leading to improved performance, reduced stress, and greater satisfaction in your role as an official.

RULE 4.2

THINK BEFORE YOU ACT—CONSEQUENCES OF EACH CALL

THE CALL

In high-stakes matches, a referee's decision acts like a stone thrown into a pond—the initial splash is just the start. Chain reactions occur when one call directly influences subsequent player behavior, fan reactions, or even future decisions you'll make. These decisions often feel instinctive, akin to reactions, but there is a critical distinction between reacting and responding. Understanding and applying this difference can empower referees to maintain control over their decision-making and enhance their performance.

Key components referees must grasp include:
Understanding the situation: Read the "temperature" of the game. For example, in a soccer match, recognizing that tensions are rising between two rival players after a series of physical challenges.
Making sense of the bigger picture: Recognize how prior decisions set behavioral precedents. For example, realizing that not calling a foul on a borderline tackle early in the game may lead to more aggressive play later.

Emotional regulation: Separate the immediate reaction from long-game implications. For example, in baseball, instead of ejecting a manager for disputing a close call, the umpire gives a firm verbal warning to maintain order and keep the manager in the game.

Consistency: Apply rules uniformly to avoid creating perceived loopholes. For example, in American football, the same standard for pass interference calls is maintained throughout the game, regardless of the score or time remaining.

The Advantage

Officials who master game rhythm gain significant benefits. They experience effortless control, where decisions become intuitive rather than forced, like a surfer riding a wave, moving with the game rather than against it. This mastery also leads to enhanced awareness, creating a heightened state of consciousness where subtle cues, often missed by others, become apparent. Time seems to slow down in crucial moments, allowing for more precise decision-making. By working with the game's flow rather than fighting it, officials conserve both mental and physical energy, finishing games feeling energized rather than exhausted.

Perhaps most importantly, this attunement to the game's rhythm fosters natural authority. Players and coaches instinctively sense when an official is in sync with the game, perceiving their decisions as natural extensions of play rather than external interruptions. This smooth integration enhances the official's credibility and command of the game.

The Penalty

Officials who fail to find rhythm face a multitude of challenges. They often find themselves in a state of perpetual struggle, fighting against the game's natural flow. This resistance is akin to swimming upstream—exhausting and ultimately futile, with every decision becoming a battle. Their inability to sync with the game's tempo frequently results in timing disruptions, where calls are made either too early or too late, creating frustration for all participants. The game becomes choppy and disjointed, preventing players from finding their own rhythm and potentially leading to a poorer quality contest with increased tensions.

When misaligned, there can be a significant mental strain on the official. When out of sync, they tend to second-guess every decision, creating a cycle of doubt and hesitation that further erodes their confidence and effectiveness. The cumulative effect is a deterioration of the official's performance and the overall quality of the game, highlighting the critical importance of mastering the art of reading and riding the game's rhythm.

The Game Plan

Reactions are immediate, automatic behaviors triggered by an event. For example, a referee might instinctively blow the whistle upon seeing contact between players without fully considering the context. While reactions are essential for quick judgments, they can sometimes lead to errors or emotional responses that compromise professionalism.

Responses, on the other hand, involve a deliberate pause—a moment to assess the situation before acting. This pause enables referees to make thoughtful decisions, ensuring accuracy and maintaining authority on the field. The ability to respond rather than react is especially valuable in managing contentious situations, such as player dissent or fan pressure.

Here's how to consider reactions and responses in relation to each other.

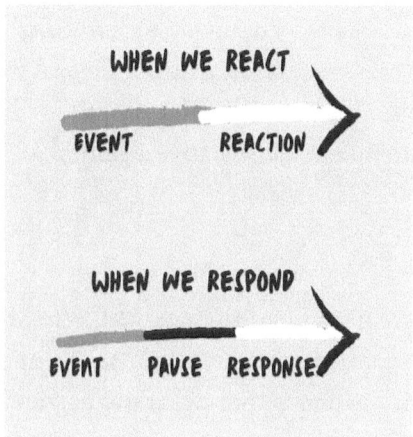

The power of the pause image highlights the importance of inserting a pause between the event and the outcome to take a reaction to a response.

For referees, this pause can take various forms:
- A deep breath to calm nerves and refocus
- Stepping back mentally or physically to gain perspective
- A quick internal check to evaluate whether action is necessary
- Engaging in self-talk to reaffirm confidence in decision-making

These techniques allow referees to shift from reactive behavior to intentional responses, fostering greater control and composure. Here are some examples of how it can apply:

Managing player dissent: A player protests a call aggressively. Instead of reacting emotionally or escalating the situation, the referee takes a breath and calmly explains the decision or uses body language to assert authority without engaging in an argument.

Handling controversial calls: In moments of doubt, such as whether a foul warrants advantage or stoppage, the referee uses the brief pause between seeing the incident and blowing the whistle to consider game dynamics and potential outcomes.

Dealing with fan pressure: Under intense crowd scrutiny, a referee might feel tempted to overcompensate or second-guess decisions. By pausing and focusing on officiating fundamentals (e.g., positioning, rule application), they can maintain objectivity and confidence.

Responding to errors: If a referee realizes they've made an incorrect call, instead of spiraling into self-criticism, they take time during a stoppage or break to reflect constructively and plan improvements for future decisions.

The art of pausing isn't limited to matchday—it can be cultivated in everyday life. Practicing deliberate responses during routine interactions builds mental resilience that naturally carries over into officiating. For instance, you might try practicing pausing before responding to heated discussions at home or work. Visualization exercises during training sessions can also simulate match scenarios where pausing leads to better judgment.

One referee reported significant improvements after adopting this strategy both on and off the field. They noted calmer decision-making during matches and enhanced relationships outside of sport, demonstrating how personal habits influence professional performance.

Reactions often feel automatic and uncontrollable, whether it's snapping at dissenting players or hesitating under pressure. By introducing a pause, referees regain control over their actions. This deliberate approach creates a sense of authority and stability even in unpredictable situations.

Ultimately, while referees cannot control every aspect of a game —such as player behavior or fan reactions—they are entirely responsible for their responses. Learning to pause transforms officiating from reactive instinct into proactive mastery, allowing referees to dictate the flow of the game with confidence and professionalism.

By integrating this mindset into their game plan, referees not only improve decision-making accuracy but also enhance their overall presence on the field, a crucial factor in earning respect from players, coaches, and spectators alike.

RULE 4.3

INFLUENCE THROUGH PRESENCE—YOUR BODY SPEAKS FIRST

The Call

Before your whistle sounds or you signal a call, your body has already communicated volumes. Presence isn't about physical size or strength—it's about occupying space with purpose and confidence. Like a conductor before an orchestra, your mere stance can command attention or invite chaos.

As an official, your presence is a powerful tool that can prevent infractions, clarify decisions, and maintain control without uttering a word. It's the silent language that speaks louder than any verbal command. When you step onto the field or court with a commanding presence, you set the tone for the entire game.

Key elements of commanding presence include positioning, movement, gesture, eye contact, and posture. Always face the action, maintaining an "open body position" that allows you to see and be seen. Your movements should be purposeful and measured, not reactive scrambling. Gestures and signals should be clear and decisive, starting and ending with precision. Eye contact should be strategic and intentional, neither avoiding nor staring. Your posture should be upright but not rigid, alert but not tense.

Mastering these elements creates an aura of authority that players, coaches, and spectators instinctively respect. It's the difference between an official who controls the game and one who merely observes it.

The Advantage

Officials who master presence gain significant benefits. They develop preventive authority, where their bearing alone deters infractions. Players think twice before testing boundaries when they sense genuine command of the space. This presence also enhances decision clarity. When your body is balanced and positioned well, your mind follows suit, leading to sharper decision-making.

Having a strong presence conserves energy. By reducing the need for verbal intervention and excessive whistle use, you'll find yourself doing more by doing less, preserving mental and physical energy for crucial moments. Perhaps most importantly, a commanding presence provides a psychological advantage. When your body projects confidence, your mind believes it, creating a positive feedback loop where presence enhances performance, which in turn strengthens presence.

The Penalty

Officials who neglect presence face several challenges. They often experience an authority deficit, playing catch-up with respect throughout the game. This can lead to compensating with excessive whistles and verbal commands, further undermining their authority. Poor presence often correlates with poor positioning, forcing you to officiate from behind the play, constantly reacting rather than controlling.

Credibility erosion is another significant risk. Even correct calls can lose impact when delivered with uncertain body language. Players and coaches unconsciously read and respond to physical cues that suggest doubt. Finally, weak presence requires constant compensation, draining your physical and mental resources prematurely and potentially impacting your performance in critical late-game situations.

The Game Plan

To enhance your presence and harness its power, implement the following techniques:

The power pose protocol: Research shows that adopting "power poses" for just two minutes can increase testosterone and decrease cortisol levels, enhancing confidence and reducing stress. Before games, find a private space and practice this technique:
- Stand tall with feet shoulder-width apart
- Raise your arms in a "V" above your head
- Hold this pose for 120 seconds
- Focus on slow, deep breathing

This simple practice can significantly boost your confidence and reduce pre-game jitters, setting the stage for a commanding presence throughout the match.

The triangle of presence: During play, implement this three-point system to maintain a strong presence:
- Base: Keep your feet shoulder-width apart, creating a stable foundation
- Core: Engage your core muscles, promoting an upright posture
- Crown: Imagine a string pulling the top of your head toward the sky

This physical alignment not only projects confidence but also improves your balance and readiness to move quickly when needed.

The 3-point presence check: During natural breaks in play, run this quick diagnostic to ensure you are maintaining a strong presence:
- Physical: Am I positioned to see both action and reaction?
- Mental: Does my body language match my authority?
- Spatial: Am I controlling my space or being controlled by others?

This regular self-assessment helps you stay aware of your presence and make adjustments as needed throughout the game.

Presence zones: Divide the field or court into presence zones:
- High presence zone: Areas of current or potential conflict where your full presence is required
- Moderate presence zone: Areas near the action where you need to be visible but not intrusive
- Observational zone: Areas away from immediate action where you can relax slightly while maintaining awareness

Move between these zones purposefully, adjusting your level of presence as needed. This approach helps you conserve energy while ensuring you are fully present when it matters most.

The presence warm-up: Incorporate presence-enhancing exercises into your pre-game routine:
- Practice your signals at full speed and intensity
- Run through a series of quick direction changes, maintaining an upright posture
- Rehearse your "game face," the neutral, alert expression you'll maintain during play

This warm-up not only prepares your body but also mentally transitions you into your officiating role.

Presence anchors: Develop physical or mental triggers to boost your presence instantly:
- A specific breath pattern
- A subtle physical gesture, like pressing your thumb and forefinger together
- A quick mental image of yourself at your most confident

Use these anchors whenever you need to enhance your presence during the game quickly.

You can use video footage or photos of yourself officiating to be curious about your language. What does the way you hold your body "say" to you and to those watching you?

By consistently applying these techniques, you'll develop a commanding presence that becomes second nature. You'll find yourself making fewer calls—not because infractions aren't occurring, but because your very bearing prevents them. Players will respond to your physical authority, coaches will respect your composed confidence, and you'll navigate even the most challenging games with greater ease.

The most effective officials aren't those who shout the loudest or blow the whistle most frequently, they're the ones whose presence alone keeps the game flowing smoothly. Master your presence, and you master the art of officiating.

Presence is not about intimidation or arrogance. It's about projecting calm authority, unwavering focus, and fair-minded confidence. Your goal is to be a stabilizing force in the game whose very bearing encourages fair play and respect for the rules.

RULE 4 IN SUMMARY
THE POWER OF THE WHISTLE RULE

Think of these three principles as puzzle pieces that fit together to help you maintain authority, focus, and composure as an official:

Rule 4.1 Control and letting go: This principle emphasizes focusing your energy on factors within your influence, such as preparation, positioning, and decision-making, while letting go of external distractions like weather or crowd reactions.

Rule 4.2 Respond not react: This principle highlights the importance of understanding how your decisions set precedents and influence player behavior, game flow, and overall dynamics.

Rule 4.3 Your presence: This principle teaches how to project calm authority and confidence through posture, movement, and non-verbal cues to manage the game effectively without over-relying on verbal commands or whistles.

Let's consider how these principles could be applied across different sports:

Soccer

Imagine a soccer referee managing a heated rivalry match. By focusing on controllable elements like positioning and staying calm under pressure (Rule 4.1), they can anticipate potential conflicts. When deciding whether to issue a yellow card for a borderline tackle (Rule 4.2), they consider how this will impact player behavior for the rest of the game. Finally, their confident body language and purposeful movement (Rule 4.3) help diffuse tensions without escalating the situation.

Basketball

In basketball, a referee might face a coach arguing over a call. By controlling their response and maintaining composure (Rule 4.1), they avoid escalating the conflict. When deciding whether to call a technical foul (Rule 4.2), they weigh the impact on game momentum. Their upright posture and steady eye contact (Rule 4.3) reinforce their authority without needing excessive verbal explanation.

Tennis

In tennis, an umpire may need to manage a player disputing a line call. By focusing on their preparation and staying calm under scrutiny (Rule 4.1), they maintain control. Their decision to uphold or overturn the call (Rule 4.2) considers its effect on match dynamics. Through clear hand signals and an assured tone (Rule 4.3.), they communicate confidence in their ruling.

RULE 4 IN SUMMARY   85

In each case, the three principles work together:
- Controlling what you can control is your anchor.
- Responding not reacting is your compass.
- Influence through presence is your shield.

When all three elements align, you create an environment where players respect your authority without question, coaches trust your ability to manage the game fairly, spectators see you as a steadying force in tense moments and you feel confident and composed in even the most challenging situations.

Remember: Control isn't about dominating every aspect of the game; it's about managing yourself so effectively that others naturally follow your lead.

To implement the learnings from Rule 4 – The Power of the Whistle download your bonus copy of *The Whistle Blower Workbook*.

Scan this QR code or visit: https://books.drjolukins.com/tn2elyoas6

RULE 5

SPLIT-SECOND CLARITY

"The difference between something good and something great is attention to detail."
—Charles R. Swindoll

IN THE WORLD OF SPORTS OFFICIATING, QUICK THINKING CAN make or break a game how quick thinking can make or break a game. Two key elements stand out: trusting your gut and being ready for anything. While we know that games can be unpredictable, it's the ability to make clear, fast decisions that sets great refs apart.

In fast-paced moments, the pressure to decide quickly can feel intense, but it's also where a referee's skills truly shine. Staying present and composed allows you to filter out distractions and focus on what matters most in the moment. This presence of mind not only helps you make accurate calls, but also builds trust with players and coaches who rely on your judgment when the game is on the line.

In Rule 5, we'll explore how to make smart calls in the blink of an eye through three key principles:

Rule 5.1: Trust Your Instincts—The Power of Decision Conviction
Rule 5.2: Mindful Presence—Being in the Moment
Rule 5.3: Focus and Process—The Art of Mental Filtering

This mental rule emphasizes the importance of clarity and quick decision-making in officiating. By trusting your instincts, staying mindfully present, and mastering the art of mental filtering, you'll be better equipped to make split-second decisions that keep the game flowing smoothly. In the dynamic environment of sports officiating, clarity of thought and action can make all the difference.

RULE 5.1

TRUST YOUR INSTINCTS—THE POWER OF DECISION CONVICTION

The Call

Your instincts as a referee are built from many hours of experience, training, and observation. Like a goalkeeper's dive or a martial artist's block, these split-second responses aren't random, they're your expertise in action. When you second-guess these instincts, you are actually questioning years of accumulated wisdom.

Consider a crucial moment in a basketball game. A defender and an offensive player collide near the basket. In that split second, you must decide: charging foul or blocking foul? There's no time for a lengthy mental debate. You must trust your instincts, make the call, and stay committed to it.

The key is understanding that commitment doesn't mean stubbornness. It means trusting your initial read while maintaining the composure to acknowledge clear errors. This balance between confidence and humility is what separates good officials from great ones.

The Advantage

Officials who trust their instincts and maintain commitment gain several key benefits:

☑ *Decision velocity*: The ability to make quick, confident calls without hesitation is crucial in fast-paced sports where even a moment's delay can impact the game's flow.

☑ *Enhanced credibility*: Players, coaches, and spectators can sense when an official is confident in their decisions. This confidence breeds respect and can often prevent arguments before they start.

☑ *Mental clarity*: When you trust your instincts, you free your mind from the burden of constant second-guessing. This clarity allows you to stay present and focused on the game as it unfolds rather than dwelling on past decisions.

☑ *Energy conservation*: The mental strain of questioning every decision is exhausting. By trusting your initial read, you preserve mental energy for when it's truly needed.

The Penalty

Officials who struggle with trust and commitment face several challenges. Decision paralysis can set in, where the fear of making a mistake leads to hesitation or indecision, resulting in missed calls or late whistles that frustrate players and disrupt the game's flow. Confidence erosion occurs when constant self-doubt becomes a self-fulfilling prophecy, with body language potentially betraying uncertainty and causing players and coaches to question your authority. This can lead to a loss of control, as participants who sense a lack of conviction are more likely to challenge calls or push boundaries. Finally, mental fatigue sets in from constantly battling one's own instincts, potentially leading to poor decision-making later in the game when clear thinking is most crucial.

The Game Plan

To master the art of trusting your instincts and staying committed, implement the quick decision toolkit. This practical approach will help you build and maintain decision conviction throughout your officiating career.

Pre-match mental rehearsal: Before each game, spend 5-10 minutes visualizing yourself making confident, quick decisions in various game scenarios. Find a quiet space and close your eyes. Imagine yourself on the field or court, facing different situations that require split-second decisions.
For example, visualize:
- A potential handball in soccer
- A close line call in tennis
- A charge/block situation in basketball

See yourself making these calls confidently and decisively. Feel the certainty in your body as you signal the decision. This mental practice primes your brain for decisive action during the actual game. More information on visualization can be found in Rule 1.3.

Pattern recognition training: Regularly review game footage to identify common patterns in play. Focus on recognizing meaningful cues that allow you to anticipate and respond effectively to game situations.
Set aside time each week to watch recordings of games in your sport. Pay attention to:
- How plays develop
- Player movements that often lead to fouls or violations
- Common scenarios that require quick decisions

As you watch, pause the video before the referee makes a call. Make your own decision, then compare it to the actual call. This practice will sharpen your ability to read the game and make quick, accurate decisions.

Post-game reflection: After each match, briefly review your key decisions. Note what went well and areas for improvement, focusing on the process rather than just the outcome.

Create a simple journal or use a notes app on your phone. After each game, spend 5-10 minutes answering these questions:

1. What were the 3-5 most crucial decisions I made today? For each decision:
2. Did I trust my initial instinct?
3. Was I able to make the call within 3 seconds?
4. How did my decision impact the game?
5. What patterns or situations do I need to study more?

This reflection helps reinforce good habits and identifies areas where you can improve your decision-making process.

Implementing the Quick Decision Toolkit
A gradual introduction of these rules will help you build your skills in making quick and effective decisions.

Week 1-2: Focus on the pre-match mental rehearsal. Make this a consistent part of your pre-game routine.

Week 3-4: Begin your pattern recognition training. Watch at least one game recording per week, focusing on decision-making moments.

Week 5-6: Start your post-game reflection practice. Keep it brief but consistent after each game.

By the end of six weeks, you should have a solid foundation in all three elements of the toolkit. Continue to practice and refine these skills throughout your officiating career.

The goal isn't to be infallible—it is to be decisive and consistent. Your instincts are a powerful tool, honed through years of experience and training. Trust them, commit to your decisions, and you'll find yourself officiating with greater clarity and confidence.

As you master this principle, you'll notice a positive cycle developing. The more you trust your instincts, the more confident you become. The more confident you are, the easier it is to make quick, decisive calls. And the more you make these quick, decisive calls, the more you reinforce your trust in your instincts.

This principle, when mastered, doesn't just improve your decision-making, it transforms your entire approach to officiating. You'll move from reacting to the game to proactively managing it. Players and coaches will sense your confidence and respond accordingly. And you'll find yourself enjoying the challenge of officiating more than ever before.

Trust your instincts, stay committed to your decisions, and watch as your officiating reaches new levels of excellence.

RULE 5.2

MINDFUL PRESENCE—BEING IN THE MOMENT

THE CALL

Maintaining focus and composure whilst officiating the game is paramount. Mindful presence is about being fully engaged in the moment, being aware of your surroundings, and feeling in control of your reactions. This principle emphasizes the importance of staying present in key moments, practicing mindfulness techniques, and maintaining a professional demeanor throughout the game.

Imagine a tennis umpire who remains perfectly composed during a heated argument with a player, or a football referee who maintains unwavering focus during a crucial play in the final seconds of a tight game. These officials embody mindful presence, demonstrating an ability to stay centered and focused regardless of external pressures or distractions.

Mindful presence is not just about concentration; it's about cultivating a state of awareness that allows you to respond to situations with clarity and purpose rather than simply reacting. It's about developing the mental resilience to handle the pressures of officiating while maintaining your professionalism and effectiveness.

The Advantage

Officials who master mindful presence gain a significant edge in their performance and decision-making abilities. They often have improved focus and concentration, allowing them to pick up on subtle details that might otherwise be missed. This heightened awareness can lead to more accurate calls and better overall game management.

These officials also tend to exhibit greater emotional control. By staying present and mindful, they're less likely to be rattled by unexpected events or confrontations. This emotional stability can have a calming effect on the entire game environment, helping to maintain order and respect even in high-pressure situations.

Officials who practice mindful presence often report reduced stress and fatigue during and after games. By staying focused on the present moment rather than worrying about past or future events, they conserve mental energy and maintain peak performance for longer periods.

Mindful presence also enhances an official's ability to make clear, unbiased decisions. By remaining fully present and aware, you are less likely to be influenced by external factors or personal biases, leading to fairer and more consistent officiating.

The Penalty

Officials who struggle with mindful presence may face a range of challenges that can undermine their effectiveness. They might find themselves easily distracted by external factors such as crowd noise or player complaints, leading to missed calls or delayed reactions. This lack of focus can result in inconsistent officiating and a loss of control over the game.

These officials may also be more susceptible to stress and emotional reactions. Without the grounding effect of mindful presence, they might react impulsively to provocations or make decisions based on emotion rather than clear judgment. This can lead to escalated conflicts and a loss of respect from players and coaches.

Furthermore, officials who can't maintain a mindful presence often experience greater mental fatigue as the game progresses. This fatigue can lead to decreased performance in crucial late-game situations when clear thinking and quick reactions are critical.

Lack of mindful presence can also manifest in poor body language or inconsistent demeanor, which can undermine an official's authority and credibility on the field. Players and coaches are quick to pick up on signs of distraction or uncertainty, which can invite challenges to your decisions.

THE GAME PLAN

To cultivate a mindful presence and enhance your officiating performance, focus on these key strategies:

1. *Develop a pre-game centering routine:* Create a short ritual to help you enter a state of mindful presence before each game. This might involve a series of deep breaths, a brief meditation, or a set of focusing exercises. The goal is to clear your mind of distractions and bring your full attention to the present moment. Practice this routine consistently so it becomes a natural part of your pre-game preparation. You can incorporate this into Rule 1.1.

2. *Practice the three-breath reset:* During natural breaks in play or moments of potential stress, use a quick breathing technique to re-center yourself. Take three slow, deep breaths, focusing your attention fully on each inhale and exhale. This simple practice can help you regain focus and composure in challenging situations. Make this reset a habit, using it regularly throughout the game to maintain your mindful presence.

3. *Use physical anchors*: Choose specific sensory cues to serve as reminders to stay present. This could be the feel of your whistle in your hand, the sound of your shoes on the court, or the sight of a particular part of the field or arena. Whenever you notice these anchors, use them as triggers to bring your attention back to the present moment. Regularly check in with these anchors throughout the game to maintain your mindful presence.

4. *Engage in post-game reflection*: After each game, take time to reflect on your level of mindful presence. Identify moments when you felt fully engaged and present, as well as times when your focus may have wavered. Consider what factors contributed to your state of mind in these situations. Use these insights to refine your approach and set specific goals for maintaining a mindful presence in future games.

You'll develop a stronger capacity for mindful presence on the field or court by consistently applying these strategies. Mindful presence is not about achieving a perfect state of concentration at all times. It's about cultivating the ability to continually bring your attention back to the present moment, regardless of distractions or pressures.

As you master this principle, you'll likely find that your officiating becomes more consistent, your decision-making clearer, and your overall presence more commanding. Mindful presence allows you to officiate from a place of calm awareness, enhancing your ability to manage the game effectively and fairly. This not only improves your performance but also contributes to a better experience for all participants in the sport.

RULE 5.3

FOCUS AND PROCESS—THE ART OF MENTAL FILTERING

THE CALL

In the chaos of competition, your ability to filter information becomes your superpower. Like a camera lens adjusting its focus, you must zoom in on crucial details while maintaining awareness of the broader picture. This skill is essential in the fast-paced world of sports officiating, where every second counts and multiple events unfold simultaneously.

Imagine a basketball referee during a fast break. In a matter of seconds, they must track the ball handler, watch for potential fouls, monitor the shot clock, and be aware of off-ball actions. The ability to quickly prioritize and process this information is what separates elite officials from the rest.

This principle is about developing the mental agility to sift through the noise and focus on what truly matters. It's about training your mind to be both a microscope and a telescope—zooming in on critical details while maintaining a broad perspective of the game.

The Advantage

Officials who master focus and processing gain significant benefits that elevate their performance. Their decision accuracy improves dramatically as they can quickly identify and analyze the most relevant information in any given situation. This leads to more consistent and fair officiating, earning the respect of players, coaches, and spectators alike.

These officials also develop superior mental endurance. By efficiently filtering information, they conserve mental energy, allowing them to maintain peak performance even in long, intense matches. This stamina is crucial in high-stakes games where concentration must be maintained until the final whistle.

Mastery of focus and processing also grants officials greater situational control. They're less likely to be caught off guard by unexpected events because they're constantly processing the game's flow and anticipating potential scenarios. This proactive approach allows them to position themselves optimally and make split-second decisions with confidence.

Officials who excel in this area achieve a remarkable emotional balance. By focusing on relevant information and filtering out distractions, they're less likely to be swayed by crowd reactions, player emotions, or personal biases. This emotional stability is the cornerstone of fair and impartial officiating.

The Penalty

Officials who struggle with focus and processing face significant challenges that can undermine their effectiveness. Information overload is a common issue, where the sheer volume of stimuli in a game environment overwhelms their decision-making capacity. This can lead to hesitation, inconsistency, and a general sense of being one step behind the action.

These officials often miss crucial moments because they're unable to distinguish between important and trivial information quickly enough. A key foul might go unnoticed because they were distracted by irrelevant player interactions elsewhere on the field or court.

Decision delays are another frequent problem. When an official can't filter and process information efficiently, they may take too long to make calls, disrupting the flow of the game and frustrating players and coaches. In fast-paced sports, even a second of hesitation can be the difference between a correct call and a missed opportunity.

Mental fatigue sets in much quicker for officials who haven't mastered this skill. The constant struggle to keep up with the game's demands drains their energy, leading to decreased performance as the match progresses. This fatigue can manifest in poor positioning, missed calls, or inconsistent rule application, all of which can significantly impact the game's outcome and the official's credibility.

The Game Plan

Mental filtering and blocking are essential skills for referees to master, especially in high-pressure environments where focus and composure are crucial. Another significant challenge referees face is dealing with criticism, which can come from players, coaches, fans, and even the media. Learning to handle criticism effectively is vital for maintaining performance and mental well-being.

Techniques for mental filtering and blocking include:
1. *Force field visualization*: Imagine an invisible force field around yourself that deflects distractions. When you perceive a distraction, visualize it hitting your force field and bouncing off, ensuring it doesn't affect your focus. This technique helps maintain a clear mental space, allowing you to focus on key game elements.
2. *Mindfulness and present moment focus*: Practice mindfulness to stay fully engaged in the current moment. This involves focusing on each play as it happens without letting past mistakes or future worries cloud your judgment. Mindfulness helps you maintain composure

and avoid overthinking, allowing you to make clear, objective decisions. By staying present, you can better recognize key cues in the game, such as player positions or rule violations, and respond accordingly.

Consistent practice is crucial for integrating mental filtering and blocking into your officiating routine. Regularly practicing these techniques during training sessions helps them become more automatic during games. This consistency also enhances mental toughness, allowing you to handle the psychological challenges of high-stakes games more effectively.

Strategies to help manage criticism effectively:
1. *Maintaining composure*: It's helpful to remain calm and composed when faced with criticism. Rudeness says far more about the person criticizing than it does about you, so as best you can, avoid taking verbal abuse personally. Experienced referees emphasize the importance of not letting criticism affect their decisions, focusing instead on enforcing the rules impartially.
2. *Thick skin and resilience*: Developing a thick skin is crucial for handling criticism without letting it impact performance. Referees should remind themselves that personal attacks are commonplace and that their role is to make fair and unbiased decisions. Resilience grows with experience. It is helpful to adopt one of my favorite phrases, "we teach people how to treat us."
3. *Constructive feedback*: While negative feedback can be challenging, constructive feedback is essential for growth. Referees should seek feedback that focuses on improving their skills rather than personal attacks. This approach helps build confidence and enhances performance over time.

After games, take time to reflect on your performance. Acknowledge mistakes and learn from them. This reflective practice helps build resilience and improves decision-making skills over time.

By mastering mental filtering, blocking distractions, and effectively dealing with criticism, referees can maintain their focus and composure under pressure. These skills are essential for officiating with clarity and confidence, ensuring that the game is managed fairly and safely. Through consistent practice and a resilient mindset, referees can navigate the challenges of their role and perform at their best, even in the most intense environments.

RULE 5 IN SUMMARY
THE SPLIT-SECOND CLARITY RULE

THINK OF THESE THREE PRINCIPLES AS PUZZLE PIECES THAT FIT together to create a foundation for quick, accurate decision-making under pressure:

Rule 5.1. Trust your instincts: This principle emphasizes the importance of trusting your expertise and making confident decisions without second-guessing yourself. Years of training and experience have honed your instincts, and this principle encourages you to rely on them.

Rule 5.2. Mindful presence: This principle focuses on staying fully present in key moments. It incorporates mindfulness techniques to maintain focus and composure, ensuring a professional demeanor throughout the game.

Rule 5.3. Focus and process: Mental filtering is your superpower. This principle teaches you how to prioritize critical information while ignoring distractions, helping you maintain clarity and control in chaotic game environments.

Let's consider how these principles could be applied across different sports:

Rugby League

In rugby league, a referee might face a split-second decision on whether a tackle was high or legal. Trusting their instincts (Rule 5.1) allows them to make the call confidently. Mindful presence (Rule 5.2) helps to dial into the decision at hand, the nuances of tackle height rules, while mental filtering (Rule 5.3) helps them focus on the point of contact amidst the chaos of a fast-moving play.

Tennis

In tennis, an umpire must decide whether a ball landed in or out during a crucial point. Trusting their instincts (Rule 5.1) enables them to make the call decisively. Mindful presence (Rule 5.2) ensures they're connected to what they saw, perhaps even replaying it momentarily in their mind and then moving forward to making the call. Mental filtering (Rule 5.3) allows them to block out crowd noise and focus solely on the ball's trajectory.

Ice Hockey

In ice hockey, a referee might need to determine whether a player's stick made illegal contact during a high-speed play. Trusting their instincts (Rule 5.1) lets them act decisively. Mindful presence (Rule 5.2) ensures they're focused on the specific play, while mental filtering (Rule 5.3) helps them track both the puck and player actions simultaneously.

In each case, the three principles work together:
- Trust your instincts is your foundation, built on years of experience and training
- Mindful presence keeps you grounded and focused on the now
- Focus and process is your lens, helping you see clearly through the chaos

When all three elements align, you create an environment where decisions are made quickly and confidently, players trust your authority and consistency, games flow smoothly without unnecessary interruptions, and you feel composed and in control, even in high-pressure moments.

Remember: Clarity isn't just about seeing what's happening—it's about knowing what matters most in the moment.

To implement the learnings from Rule 5 – Split-Second Clarity, download your bonus copy of *The Whistle Blower Workbook*.

Scan this QR code or visit: https://books.drjolukins.com/tn2elyoas6

RULE 6

COMMAND, CONNECT, AND FOCUS

"Communication is not about speaking what we think. Communication is about ensuring others hear what we mean."
—Simon Sinek

EFFECTIVE COMMUNICATION IS THE CORNERSTONE OF successful officiating. This rule explores the layered nature of communication in officiating and its crucial role in maintaining control, building rapport with players and coaches, and staying focused throughout the game.

Clear communication goes beyond your words—it includes your tone of voice, body language, and even your ability to listen under pressure. When referees communicate confidently and consistently, it helps diffuse tension, prevents misunderstandings, and sets a positive tone for interactions on the court. This supports fair play and strengthens your authority and presence throughout the game.

Within Rule 6, we will explore the art of communication and how it fundamentally impacts your officiating performance.

Rule 6.1: Clear and Confident Communication—The Voice of Authority
Rule 6.2: Non-Verbal Communication—The Unspoken Language
Rule 6.3: Adaptive Communication—Flexibility in Action

This mental rule emphasizes the power of effective communication in officiating. By mastering various communication techniques, you enhance your ability to command respect, connect with game participants, and maintain focus, ensuring smoother game management and increased credibility as an official.

In officiating, how you communicate can be just as important as the decisions you make. Your words, actions, and presence all contribute to your effectiveness on the field or court.

RULE 6.1

CLEAR AND CONFIDENT COMMUNICATION—THE VOICE OF AUTHORITY

THE CALL

Your ability to communicate clearly and confidently can distinguish between a well-managed game and chaos on the field. This principle is about mastering the art of verbal communication, knowing when to speak, what to say, and how to say it with authority and clarity.

Imagine a crucial moment in a baseball game. The bases are loaded, it's the bottom of the ninth, and you've just called the batter out on strikes to end the game. The losing team's manager storms out of the dugout, demanding an explanation. Your ability to communicate your decision clearly and confidently in this heated moment can defuse or escalate the situation.

Clear and confident communication is not just about being loud or assertive. It's about conveying information effectively, explaining decisions when necessary, and knowing when silence is the most powerful response. It's about striking the right balance between authority and approachability, ensuring that your words carry weight without creating unnecessary tension.

The Advantage

Officials who master clear and confident communication gain the power to enhance their overall effectiveness. Their clear instructions and explanations leave little room for misunderstanding or dispute, resulting in smoother game management. This clarity often prevents conflicts before they arise, as players and coaches are less likely to challenge decisions they clearly understand.

These officials also build stronger rapport with game participants. When officials can confidently articulate their decisions and explain them when appropriate, they foster a sense of transparency and fairness. This can increase players' and coaches' trust and respect, even when they disagree with a call.

Clear and confident communicators often find that they have better control over the game's emotional temperature. Their ability to deliver calm, authoritative explanations in tense moments can de-escalate potential conflicts and keep the game flowing smoothly. This skill is particularly valuable in high-pressure situations where emotions are running high.

Mastering this principle also contributes to an official's overall presence and authority on the field. When your words are clear, concise, and delivered confidently, it reinforces your role as the arbiter of the game. This can have a ripple effect, influencing how players and coaches interact with you throughout the match.

The Penalty

Officials who struggle with clear and confident communication face several challenges that can undermine their effectiveness. They may frequently be misunderstood, leading to unnecessary arguments and game delays. Unclear explanations can create confusion and frustration among players and coaches, potentially escalating minor disagreements into major conflicts.

Lack of confidence in communication can also erode an official's authority. They may appear uncertain or hesitant when delivering decisions or explaining things, and calls may be challenged. Coaches are quick to pick up on any sign of doubt, which leads to increased scrutiny of your choices throughout the game.

Furthermore, officials who can't communicate effectively may resort to over-explaining or arguing, disrupting the game flow and creating an adversarial atmosphere. On the other hand, those who shy away from necessary explanations might be perceived as aloof or unapproachable, damaging their rapport with game participants.

In high-pressure situations, poor communication can exacerbate tensions rather than defuse them. An inability to clearly and confidently address concerns in critical moments can lead to a loss of control, potentially affecting the outcome of the game and the overall experience for all involved.

The Game Plan

To master the art of clear and confident communication, implement the following strategies:

1. *Develop your officiating voice*: Your "officiating voice" should be distinct from your everyday speaking voice. It should be clear, authoritative, and projecting without shouting.
- Practice projecting your voice from your diaphragm, not your throat. This allows you to speak loudly without straining your voice.
- Work on enunciating clearly, especially when making calls or giving explanations.
- Record yourself making calls and listen to how you sound. Pay attention to clarity, tone, and confidence.

2. *Master the three C's—Clear, Concise, Confident*: Every verbal interaction should embody these three qualities.
Clear: Use simple, unambiguous language and avoid jargon
Concise: Get to the point quickly. In most situations, less is more.
Confident: Speak with authority, even if you're not feeling 100% sure.

Practice crafting responses to common scenarios that embody these three C's. For example, "saying Out of bounds, red ball" instead of "I think it might have gone out off the blue player."

3. *The explanation framework*: Develop a mental framework for when and how to explain decisions when asked respectfully by a player or coach, to prevent misunderstandings that could escalate, to educate on lesser-known rules.
- State the outcome
- Cite the relevant rule
- Describe what you saw (briefly)
- Restate the outcome

An example could be, "The runner is out. A runner is out when he runs more than three feet away from his baseline to avoid being tagged. I saw the runner veer outside the baseline as the fielder attempted to apply the tag. Therefore, the runner is out."

4. *The power of silence*: Recognize that sometimes, the most powerful communication is no communication at all.
- After making a call, resist the urge to over-explain unless asked
- When faced with emotional reactions, allow a brief moment of silence before responding
- Use strategic pauses in your speech to emphasize important points

Practice incorporating deliberate silences into your communication during training or lower-stakes games.

5. *Active listening techniques*: Effective communication is a two-way street. Enhance your listening skills to improve overall communication.
- Practice maintaining eye contact when someone is speaking to you.
- Use non-verbal cues (like nodding) to show you're listening.
- Resist the urge to interrupt or formulate your response while others are speaking.

6. *Post-game analysis*: After each game, reflect on your communication:
- Identify moments where your communication was particularly effective or ineffective.
- Note any situations where you wish you had communicated differently.
- Seek feedback from colleagues or mentors specifically about your communication style.

7. *Continuous improvement*: Make clear and confident communication a focus of your ongoing development.
- Attend communication workshops or public speaking classes to refine your skills.
- Study videos of elite officials, paying attention to how they communicate in various situations.
- Practice your officiating voice and calls regularly, even outside of games.

Clear and confident communication is a skill that improves with conscious effort and practice. By consistently applying these strategies, you'll develop a communication style that enhances your authority, builds trust with game participants, and contributes to smoother, more enjoyable games for all involved.

As you master this principle, you'll find that your words carry more weight, your presence on the field becomes more commanding, and your ability to manage difficult situations improves dramatically. Clear and confident communication is not just about making yourself heard—it's about making every word count in service of a fair and well-managed game.

RULE 6.2

NONVERBAL COMMUNICATION—THE UNSPOKEN LANGUAGE

THE CALL

In sports officiating, what you don't say can be just as important as what you do say. Nonverbal communication—your body language, facial expressions, and even your positioning on the field—speaks volumes about your authority, attentiveness, and control of the game. This principle focuses on mastering the silent language of officiating, ensuring that every gesture and movement reinforces your decisions and commands respect from players and coaches.

Imagine a football referee who maintains unwavering eye contact with a coach during a heated discussion or a tennis umpire whose posture exudes calm authority even as a player challenges a call. These officials understand that their non-verbal cues are powerful tools for maintaining order and respect on the field of play.

Nonverbal communication encompasses three key elements: body language that conveys authority, the art of active listening, and maintaining visual focus on your primary coverage area. Each component plays a crucial role in your overall effectiveness as an official.

The Advantage

Officials who master non-verbal communication gain a significant edge in game management. They often find that they can control situations with a look or a gesture, reducing the need for verbal interventions and keeping the game flowing smoothly. This silent authority can be particularly effective in noisy environments or across language barriers, making it an invaluable skill for officials at all levels.

These officials also tend to command more respect from players and coaches. When your body language consistently projects confidence and control, participants are less likely to challenge your decisions or authority. This can lead to fewer confrontations and a more positive game atmosphere overall.

Officials skilled in nonverbal communication often demonstrate superior situational awareness. By mastering active listening and focusing on their primary coverage area, they can better anticipate potential issues and position themselves optimally for upcoming plays. This proactive approach can significantly enhance the accuracy and timeliness of their calls.

Effective nonverbal communication can help officials maintain their composure in high-pressure situations. By focusing on controlled, purposeful movements and expressions, officials can project calm even when internal stress levels are high. This outward composure can stabilize the entire game environment.

The Penalty

Officials who struggle with nonverbal communication may face a range of challenges. Inconsistent or weak body language can undermine verbal instructions and decisions, leading to confusion among players and coaches. This can result in more frequent challenges to calls and a general erosion of the official's authority on the field.

Poor active listening skills can cause officials to miss crucial information or cues from players, coaches, or fellow officials. This can lead to misunderstandings, delayed responses to developing situations, or missed calls, which, over time, can damage the official's credibility and ability to manage the game effectively.

Officials who fail to maintain visual focus on their primary coverage area may find themselves out of position for key plays or missing important off-ball actions, potentially impacting the fairness and flow of the game. It may also increase the physical and mental strain on the officials as they constantly try to catch up with the play.

Furthermore, inconsistent or negative nonverbal cues can create an atmosphere of tension or uncertainty on the field. If an official's body language suggests doubt, anxiety, or aggression, it can heighten emotions among players and coaches, potentially escalating conflicts and disrupting the game's flow.

The Game Plan

To master the art of nonverbal communication, implement the following strategies:

1. *Body language mastery*: Develop a repertoire of non-verbal cues that project authority and control.
- Practice the "power pose": Stand tall with your feet shoulder-width apart, shoulders back, and chin up. Hold this pose for two minutes before games to boost confidence.
- Master the "neutral face": Develop a default expression that is alert and attentive but not emotional. Practice this in a mirror until it feels natural.
- Use deliberate hand gestures: Ensure your signals are crisp, clear, and decisive.
Practice these regularly to make them second nature.

2. *The active listening triad*: Implement these three components of active listening:
- Eye contact: Maintain appropriate eye contact when interacting with players or coaches. This shows engagement and commands respect.
- Body orientation: Turn your body towards the speaker, showing that you give them your full attention.
- Responsive nodding: Use subtle nods to acknowledge that you're listening, without necessarily agreeing.

3. *The nonverbal toolkit*: Develop a set of nonverbal tools for common officiating scenarios:
- The "calm down" gesture: A subtle, palms-down motion to de-escalate tensions without stopping play.
- The "I'm watching" look: A focused gaze that lets players know you're aware of developing situations.
- The "proximity control" technique: This involves moving closer to potential trouble spots without directly engaging, using your presence to maintain order.

Practice these in training sessions and gradually implement them in games.

4. *Situational body language*: Adapt your nonverbal cues to different game situations:
- High-tension moments: Project calm through slow, deliberate movements and controlled breathing.
- Routine calls: Use confident, assertive gestures to reinforce your decisions.
- Explanatory situations: Adopt an open, receptive posture when clarifying calls to players or coaches.

Role-play these situations with colleagues to refine your approach.

5. *Cultural awareness*: Recognize that nonverbal cues can have different meanings in different cultures.
- Research common nonverbal differences in cultures relevant to your officiating context.
- Be mindful of potentially offensive gestures and adapt your nonverbal toolkit accordingly.
- When officiating in unfamiliar cultural contexts, observe and mimic the nonverbal styles of respected local officials.

6. *Self-management through nonverbals*: Use nonverbal techniques to manage your own stress and project calm.
- Develop a subtle "reset" gesture when you feel tension rising.
- Practice deep, controlled breathing that's not visible to others but helps maintain your composure.
- Use power poses during breaks to recharge your confidence.

By consistently applying these strategies, you'll develop a powerful nonverbal presence that complements and enhances verbal communication. Your body is always speaking—make sure it's saying what you want it to say. As you master non-verbal communication, you'll find that you can control the game more effectively, build stronger relationships with players and coaches, and navigate challenging situations with greater ease and authority.

RULE 6.3

ADAPTIVE COMMUNICATION—FLEXIBILITY IN ACTION

The Call

In the dynamic world of sports officiating, one-size-fits-all communication rarely suffices. Adapting your communication style to the ever-changing context of a game is a crucial skill that separates great officials from good ones. This principle focuses on developing the flexibility to adjust your communication approach based on the situation, the individuals involved, and the overall temperature of the game.

Imagine an ice hockey referee transitioning from a stern warning to a player about rough play to a calm, reasoned explanation to a coach about a complex rule interpretation. Or picture a baseball umpire who can read the rising tensions in a close game and adjust their communication style to maintain control without escalating conflicts. These officials understand that effective communication is not just about what you say but how you say it in the context of the moment.

Adaptive communication encompasses three key elements: adjusting your communication style as needed, assessing the game's temperature and timing, and managing momentum through effective communication. Each component is vital in maintaining control and facilitating a fair, enjoyable game.

THE ADVANTAGE

Officials who master adaptive communication are remarkable at navigating the complex social dynamics of sporting events. They often find that they can defuse tense situations more easily, as they can choose the most effective communication approach for each unique scenario. This adaptability allows them to maintain control of the game without resorting to overly authoritarian measures that might escalate conflicts.

These officials also build better rapport with players and coaches over time. By tailoring their communication style to different personalities and situations, they demonstrate empathy and understanding, which can foster respect even in disagreement. This improved relationship with game participants often leads to smoother game management and fewer confrontations.

When skilled in adaptive communication, officials are better equipped to manage a game's overall flow and momentum. They can sense when to use communication to speed up play, when to slow things down to cool tensions, and how to maintain the right energy level throughout the contest. This ability to "read the room" and respond appropriately can significantly enhance the quality and enjoyment of the game for all involved.

In addition, adaptive communication allows officials to maintain authority more effectively across various situations. Whether dealing with a rookie player nervous about their first game or a veteran coach known for their fiery temper, these officials can consistently adjust their approach to command respect and compliance.

The Penalty

Officials who struggle with adaptive communication may face various challenges that can undermine their effectiveness. They might apply a communication style that works well in one situation to another where it's inappropriate, potentially escalating conflicts or creating unnecessary tension. For example, they might use a stern, authoritative tone when a softer approach is more effective or take a casual approach in a situation that calls for firmness.

These officials may also have difficulty managing the emotional temperature of a game. Without the ability to adjust their communication style, they might inadvertently increase tensions during critical moments or fail to assert control when necessary. This can lead to losing game control, with players and coaches potentially taking advantage of the official's inflexibility.

Furthermore, officials who can't adapt their communication styles may struggle to build positive relationships with game participants over time. Players and coaches may perceive them as rigid or unresponsive to the nuances of different situations, potentially increasing challenges to their authority and decisions.

The inability to adapt communication can also result in missed opportunities to educate players and coaches about rules or to prevent infractions before they occur. This can lead to a more punitive style of officiating rather than one that facilitates fair play and understanding.

The Game Plan

To master the art of adaptive communication, focus on these key strategies:

1. *Implement the temperature check technique*: Regularly assess the emotional climate of the game to inform your communication approach. Develop a mental "temperature scale" from 1 (very calm) to 10 (extremely tense). Perform quick assessments at natural breaks in play and adjust your communication style based on the current "tem-

perature." This will help you stay in tune with the game's emotional state and respond appropriately.

2. *Maintain a feedback loop*: Continuously refine your adaptive communication skills through feedback and reflection. After each game, reflect on key communication moments and their effectiveness. Seek input from colleagues or mentors about your communication style. Use this feedback to adjust and expand your adaptive strategies. This ongoing process of reflection and improvement will help you continually enhance your adaptive communication skills.

Remember, the goal of adaptive communication is not to be chameleon-like, changing your fundamental character, but to have the flexibility to choose the most effective approach for each unique situation. As you master this principle, you'll find you can navigate even the most challenging officiating scenarios with greater ease and effectiveness, leading to smoother, more enjoyable games for everyone involved.

RULE 6 IN SUMMARY
THE COMMAND, CONNECT, AND FOCUS RULE

Think of these three principles as puzzle pieces that fit together to create a foundation for effective communication, ensuring smoother game management and greater respect from participants:

Rule 6.1. Clear and confident communication: This principle emphasizes the importance of delivering messages clearly and authoritatively. It focuses on being concise, explaining decisions when necessary, and recognizing when silence is the most effective response.

Rule 6.2. Nonverbal communication: This principle highlights how body language, facial expressions, and positioning convey authority and attentiveness. It also stresses the importance of active listening and focusing on your primary coverage area.

Rule 6.3. Adaptive communication: This principle teaches you to adjust your communication style based on the situation. It involves assessing the emotional temperature of the game, managing momentum shifts, and tailoring your approach to different personalities.

Let's think about how these principles could be applied across different sports:
Handball
In handball, an official must communicate decisions about fouls or penalties (Rule 6.1) while using confident body language to reinforce their calls (Rule 6.2). Adaptive communication (Rule 6.3) helps manage player emotions as tensions rise in a dynamic match.

Baseball
In a baseball game, the umpires use clear and concise signals for strikes or outs (Rule 6.1). Their nonverbal cues include a steady posture behind home plate (Rule 6.2) and projecting authority. Adaptive communication (Rule 6.3) is also important when managing interactions with coaches during disputes.

Ice hockey
Referees must communicate penalties over loudspeakers or with hand signals (Rule 6.1). Their body language during face-offs or after physical plays (Rule 6.2) conveys control. Adaptive communication (Rule 6.3) helps manage heated exchanges between players.

In each case, the three principles work together:
- Clear and confident words carry authority
- Nonverbal communication is your silent tool
- Adaptive communication is your flexibility

When all three elements align, you create an environment where players trust your authority and decisions, coaches respect your ability to manage the game fairly, games flow smoothly without unnecessary interruptions, and you feel confident and in control throughout the match.

Remember: Communication isn't just about what you say—it's about how you connect with those around you to create clarity, respect, and flow.

To implement the learnings from Rule 6 – Command, Connect and Focus, download your bonus copy of *The Whistle Blower Workbook*.

Scan this QR code or visit: https://books.drjolukins.com/tn2elyoas6

PART 3
MENTAL RESILIENCE

THE MENTAL ASPECT OF OFFICIATING IS WHAT SEPARATES GOOD officials from great ones. This section delves into the critical components of mental resilience that enable you to perform at your best, even under intense pressure and scrutiny. We'll explore three key rules to help you develop the mental fortitude necessary to thrive in challenging situations.

These pages will uncover the power of your inner voice, the art of quick recovery, and the ability to harness pressure to your advantage. These elements are crucial for building mental toughness and maintaining peak performance throughout your officiating career.

Rule 7: Discover Your Inner Coach

Learn to harness the power of positive self-talk, transforming your inner dialogue into a source of strength and motivation during crucial moments.

Rule 8: The Bounce-Back Blueprint

Develop strategies to quickly recover from setbacks, maintaining your effectiveness and composure throughout the game.

Rule 9: Pressure Points
Discover techniques to embrace pressure, turning high-stakes situations into opportunities for peak performance rather than sources of stress.

Integrating these rules into your officiating approach will help you develop the mental resilience needed to excel in even the most challenging environments.

Remember: Mental toughness is not about never feeling pressure or doubt, it's about responding to challenges.

RULE 7

DISCOVER YOUR INNER COACH

"When I am right, no one remembers. When I am wrong, no one forgets."
—Doug Harvey

YOUR INNER VOICE IS ONE OF THE MOST INFLUENTIAL TOOLS IN your officiating arsenal. Depending on how you engage with it, it can either build you up or tear you down. This rule focuses on transforming your inner dialogue into a constructive and empowering force that supports your performance, even in the most challenging moments.

By becoming more aware of your self-talk, you can start to notice patterns that either help or hinder your confidence on the court. When you consciously replace negative or doubtful thoughts with positive, realistic affirmations, you lay the groundwork for greater resilience and sharper decision-making. Over time, this constructive inner dialogue becomes a reliable source of support, helping you stay composed and focused no matter what challenges arise during a game.

Within Rule 7, we will explore how to harness the power of your inner voice to enhance confidence, resilience, and focus. You can maintain composure under pressure and continually grow as an official by learning to coach yourself effectively from within.

Rule 7.1: Positive Self-Talk—The Power of Helpful Thinking
Rule 7.2: Constructive Self-Reflection—Learning from Experience
Rule 7.3: Mental Reset Techniques—Regain Your Focus

This mental rule emphasizes the transformative power of inner dialogue. You can create a strong internal foundation that supports your officiating performance and resilience by mastering positive self-talk, constructive self-reflection, and mental reset techniques.

Your inner voice is always with you—make it a coach who inspires confidence, growth, and excellence.

In my book *Belief: Building Unshakeable Confidence*, I explore the concept of the Inner Coach, a powerful internal dialogue that can help you cultivate unwavering confidence. This Inner Coach serves as your mental guide, offering supportive commentary to strengthen your belief in yourself. If you'd like to find out more about Belief, scan this QR code or visit: https://www.drjolukins.com/belief

RULE 7.1

POSITIVE SELF-TALK—THE POWER OF HELPFUL THINKING

The Call

In the high-pressure world of sports officiating, your inner voice can be your greatest ally or worst enemy. Positive self-talk is about harnessing the power of your internal dialogue to boost confidence, maintain focus, and overcome challenges. It is consciously replacing negative thoughts with encouraging and empowering ones.

Imagine you are a tennis umpire facing a contentious line call in a Grand Slam final. The crowd is restless, the players are on edge, and you feel the weight of the moment. In this crucial instance, your inner voice saying, "I've trained for this. I trust my judgment," can make all the difference in maintaining your composure and making the right call.

Positive self-talk isn't about ignoring reality or pretending everything is perfect. It's about framing situations in a way that empowers you to perform at your best, even under intense scrutiny and pressure.

The Advantage

Officials who master positive self-talk experience many benefits that significantly enhance their performance. They often report increased confidence in their decision-making, as their inner voice reinforces their training and experience rather than undermining it. This confidence is powerful and can influence how players and coaches perceive and interact with you.

Maintaining focus and composure in challenging situations can be well assisted with helpful and positive self-talk When faced with a difficult call or an angry coach, officials who use positive self-talk are better equipped to stay calm and think clearly, leading to more accurate decisions and better game management.

Another key advantage is improved resilience. Officials who engage in positive self-talk tend to bounce back more quickly from mistakes or setbacks. Instead of dwelling on errors, they can learn from them and move forward, maintaining their effectiveness throughout the game.

The Penalty

Officials struggling with positive self-talk often face significant challenges that undermine their performance. Negative self-talk can erode confidence, leading to hesitation in decision-making and a tendency to second-guess calls. Players and coaches often notice this lack of decisiveness, potentially inviting more challenges to the official's authority.

Furthermore, a negative inner voice can exacerbate stress and anxiety, making it harder to stay focused and composed during crucial moments. This can lead to a downward spiral where each mistake or difficult situation further reinforces negative thoughts, potentially affecting the official's overall performance and enjoyment of their role.

When you are caught in patterns of negative self-talk, you may also struggle with resilience. A mistake or a challenging interaction can linger in your mind, affecting your confidence and decision-making for the rest of the game, or even longer. This can lead to inconsistent officiating and difficulty maintaining the high standards required at competitive levels.

THE GAME PLAN

To harness the power of positive self-talk and transform your inner voice into a supportive officiating coach, implement the following strategies:

1. *Identify and challenge negative thoughts*: Start by becoming aware of your inner dialogue, especially during challenging moments. When you notice negative thoughts, challenge them with evidence-based positive alternatives. For example, if you think, "I always struggle with this type of call," reframe it to, "I've handled similar situations successfully before, and I'm well-prepared for this."

2. *Develop a positive affirmation toolkit*: Create a set of positive affirmations tailored to different officiating scenarios. These might include:
   "I am well-prepared and confident in my abilities."
   "I trust my judgment and make decisions with clarity."
   "I remain calm and focused, even under pressure."
   Practice these affirmations regularly during games and daily life to make them a natural part of your inner dialogue.

3. *Use the "I will" technique*: Replace phrases like "I can't" or "I hope" with "I will." This simple shift can significantly impact your mindset and approach to challenges. For instance, instead of thinking, "I hope

I don't mess up this call," affirm, "I will make this call accurately and confidently."

4. *Implement a pre-game mental routine*: Develop a short pre-game ritual that includes positive self-talk. This may involve repeating your key affirmations, visualizing successful officiating scenarios, or taking a few deep breaths while reminding yourself of your capabilities. This routine can help set a positive tone for your inner dialogue throughout the game.

5. *Practice self-compassion*: Treat yourself with the same kindness and understanding you would offer a colleague or friend. When you make a mistake, acknowledge it without harsh self-criticism. Instead, use supportive language like, "I'm learning from this and will do better next time."

6. *Use trigger words or phrases*: Identify short, powerful words or phrases that can quickly reset your mindset during a game. These might be words like "focus," "confident," or "present." Use these triggers whenever you need a quick mental boost or refocus.

7. *Conduct post-game positive reviews*: After each game, take time to reflect on what went well. Identify specific moments where you demonstrated skill, composure, or good judgment. This practice reinforces positive self-talk and builds confidence for future games.

You'll gradually transform your inner voice into a supportive and empowering force by consistently applying these strategies. Remember, positive self-talk is a skill that improves with practice. Be patient with yourself as you develop this new habit, and celebrate the progress you make along the way.

As you master this principle, you'll likely find that your confidence grows and your resilience strengthens. Your inner voice becomes a trusted ally, guiding you through challenges and helping you perform at your best, even in the most pressure-filled moments.

RULE 7.2

CONSTRUCTIVE SELF-REFLECTION— LEARNING FROM EXPERIENCE

THE CALL

In sports officiating, it is crucial to objectively and constructively reflect on your performance. Constructive self-reflection is about turning your inner critic into an inner coach, acknowledging mistakes without dwelling on them, and using every experience to grow. This principle is the foundation of continuous improvement and resilience in officiating.

Imagine you're a rugby referee who made a controversial call in a high-stakes match. The players are frustrated, the crowd is booing, and you're starting to doubt yourself. In this moment, your ability to reflect constructively rather than criticize yourself harshly can make all the difference in handling the rest of the game and learning from the experience.

Constructive self-reflection isn't about ignoring mistakes or sugarcoating poor performance. It's about approaching your officiating with a performance mindset, and seeing challenges as opportunities to learn and improve rather than as failures or shortcomings.

The Advantage

Officials who master constructive self-reflection gain several significant benefits. They show rapid improvement in their skills, constantly learning from their experiences and applying those lessons to future games. This continuous performance mindset can lead to increased confidence and competence over time.

Further, officials with the skills to self-reflect often demonstrate greater emotional resilience. By approaching mistakes as learning opportunities rather than personal failures, they can maintain their composure and effectiveness throughout a game, even after making a difficult or controversial call.

Another key advantage is increased self-awareness. Officials who engage in constructive self-reflection develop a clearer understanding of their strengths and areas for improvement. This self-knowledge allows you to focus your training and development efforts more effectively, accelerating your progress as an official.

The Penalty

Officials struggling with constructive self-reflection often face challenges that hinder their performance and development. They may fall into patterns of harsh self-criticism, which can erode confidence and lead to hesitation in decision-making. Players and coaches can perceive this lack of confidence, potentially undermining the official's authority on the field.

Without constructive self-reflection, officials may miss valuable opportunities for growth and improvement. They might repeat the same mistakes or fail to address weaknesses in their officiating, leading to stagnation in their skills and potentially limiting their career progression.

Officials who can't reflect constructively may also struggle with resilience. A mistake or a challenging game can have a lasting negative impact on their confidence and performance, as they lack the tools to process these experiences in a healthy, growth-oriented way.

The Game Plan

Following every performance, it is helpful to remember that success leaves clues, and disappointments offer lessons. High-performance officials understand that improvement comes from understanding the clues to success and learning from the lessons. Begin by implementing a structured post-game review process. After each game, set aside time for reflection, using consistent questions to guide your analysis. This structured approach ensures that you consistently examine your performance in a balanced, constructive way.

As you engage in this reflection process, work on developing a performance mindset vocabulary. Replace fixed mindset phrases with performance-oriented alternatives. This shift in language can profoundly impact your approach to challenges and mistakes, reinforcing the idea that every experience is an opportunity for learning and improvement. For example:

> I made a bad call; I'm a terrible referee.

> That was a tough call; let me review it and see how I can do better next time.

> If I make a mistake, everyone will think I'm incompetent.

> Mistakes happen; what matters is how I respond and learn from them.

> [Name of player/coach] will be there today, he/she is always argumentative.

> [Name of player/coach] may have strong opinions, I'll deal with that as it happens.

> I'll never be as good as that other referee; they're naturally better.

> I'll focus on improving my communication skills to manage the game more effectively.

> I've been refereeing for years; I don't need to learn new rules or techniques.

> Even with experience, there's always room to improve. I'll attend workshops to stay updated on new rules and strategies.

> Feedback is criticism; I don't need it.

> Feedback is essential for growth; I'll actively seek it out to improve my performance.

A further strategy you can try is to use "what, so what, now what" framework to deepen your analysis of specific incidents or decisions. This approach helps you move from objective observation to meaningful analysis and actionable planning. It's a powerful tool for extracting valuable lessons from each officiating experience. Here are some examples:

WHAT: *A player disputes a call, claiming it was incorrect.*

So WHAT: The dispute affects the game's momentum and player morale. It also tests my ability to manage conflict.

Now WHAT: I will review the play to ensure accuracy and communicate clearly with the player to resolve the issue.

WHAT: *There was a miscommunication between me and another official regarding a penalty.*

So WHAT: This could lead to confusion and undermine the credibility of the officiating team.

Now WHAT: I will clarify the situation with the other official immediately and ensure we are on the same page moving forward.

WHAT: *A coach is pressuring me to make certain calls.*

So WHAT: This pressure can affect my impartiality and decision-making.

Now WHAT: I will maintain my composure, remind the coach of the rules regarding communication, and focus on making fair calls based on the game's situation.

WHAT: *I missed a critical call that impacted the game's outcome.*

So WHAT: Missing such calls can erode trust in my officiating abilities and affect the game's fairness.

Now WHAT: I will review the footage to understand what happened, discuss it with peers or mentors for feedback, and work on improving my focus and reaction time in similar situations.

While self-reflection is primarily an internal process, don't underestimate the value of external perspectives. Regularly seek feedback from mentors, fellow officials, or even trusted players and coaches. Comparing their observations with your reflections can provide a more comprehensive view of your performance and highlight blind spots in your self-assessment.

By weaving these strategies into your regular officiating practice, you'll develop a habit of constructive self-reflection that supports your growth and resilience as an official. The goal isn't to achieve perfection, but to cultivate a mindset of continuous improvement and learning. As you master this principle, you'll likely become more adaptable, resilient, and confident in officiating. Your inner voice will transform from a harsh critic to a supportive coach guiding you through every challenge on the field.

RULE 7.3

MENTAL RESET TECHNIQUES—REGAIN YOUR FOCUS

THE CALL

In the dynamic world of sports officiating, the ability to quickly reset your mind after each call is crucial. Mental reset techniques are about developing strategies to maintain a positive mindset throughout the game, regardless of what has transpired. This principle focuses on mental agility, allowing you to approach each new play or decision with a clear and focused mind.

Imagine you're a cricket umpire who has just made a controversial LBW decision. The batsman is visibly upset, the fielding team is elated, and the crowd is divided. At this moment, your ability to mentally reset, letting go of the previous decision and focusing entirely on the next ball, separates elite officials from the rest.

Mental reset techniques don't involve forgetting or dismissing what has happened. Instead, they include acknowledging each moment, learning from it if necessary, and then consciously shifting your focus to the present and future. This skill allows you to maintain consistency and fairness throughout the match, unaffected by past events or anticipation of future challenges.

The ability to reset is important after any decision (great or otherwise). By resetting, we help ourselves remain in the preferred *time zone* instead of the past. Practicing this rule will help you implement rule 3.3.

The Advantage

Officials who master mental reset techniques gain several significant benefits. They often demonstrate remarkable consistency in their decision-making, as each call is made with a fresh perspective, unencumbered by previous events. This consistency builds trust with players and coaches, who rely on the official's steady presence throughout the game.

Greater mental endurance is evident in officials with the ability to mentally reset. By regularly clearing their mental slate, they avoid the cumulative stress and fatigue that can come from carrying the weight of every decision throughout a long match. This mental freshness allows them to maintain peak performance, even in the crucial final moments of a game.

Another key advantage is improved focus and presence. Officials skilled in mental resets are fully engaged in each moment, which can lead to more accurate calls and better overall game management. Their ability to be present enhances their awareness of the game's flow and potential issues, allowing for more proactive officiating.

The Penalty

Officials struggling with mental reset techniques often face challenges that undermine their performance. They may dwell on past decisions, second-guessing a controversial call or basking too long in the glow of a well-handled situation. This mental stagnation can lead to missed calls or delayed reactions, as their attention is split between past events and the current play.

Without effective reset techniques, officials may become more susceptible to emotional carryover. A confrontation with a player or coach earlier in the game might influence later decisions, compromising the fairness and consistency of their officiating. This can erode trust and respect from game participants, potentially escalating tensions on the field, and leading to higher stress levels and mental fatigue as the game progresses.

The Game Plan

There are several key strategies you can integrate into your officiating practice to develop effective mental reset techniques and maintain a positive mindset throughout the game:

1. *Develop a quick reset ritual.* You can use this strategy between plays or during natural breaks in the game. This might involve a specific breathing pattern, a physical gesture like adjusting your whistle, or a brief visualization of a calm, focused state. Practice this ritual regularly so it becomes second nature, allowing you to trigger a mental reset quickly and efficiently when needed.

2. *Incorporate positive self-talk into your reset routine.* Develop a set of short, empowering phrases that you can use to refocus your mind. These might include affirmations like "Next play," "Fresh start," or "Stay present." One of my favorites is W.I.N.—What's Important Now? This is a great phrase for helping you to orient your thinking to the present. Use these phrases consistently to reinforce a positive, forward-looking mindset.

3. *Develop a strategy for handling particularly challenging or controversial moments.* This might involve a slightly longer reset process, using the break between plays to take a few deep breaths,

mentally reaffirming your expertise, and consciously letting go of any lingering emotions or doubts.

After the game, reflect on how effectively you used your reset techniques. Identify moments where you successfully cleared your mind and refocused, as well as instances where you struggled to reset. Use these insights to refine your approach and set specific goals for improvement in future games.

By consistently applying and refining these strategies, you'll develop the ability to maintain a clear, focused mind throughout even the most challenging matches. Remember, mental reset techniques are a skill that improves with practice. Be patient with yourself as you develop this ability, and celebrate the moments when you successfully navigate difficult situations with a fresh, positive mindset.

As you master this principle, you'll likely find that your officiating becomes more consistent, your mental endurance improves, and your enjoyment of the role increases. Your ability to approach each moment with clarity and focus will enhance your performance and contribute to a smoother, fairer game for all participants.

RULE 7 IN SUMMARY
THE DISCOVER YOUR INNER COACH RULE

THINK OF THESE THREE PRINCIPLES AS PUZZLE PIECES THAT FIT together to create a powerful internal support system for officiating excellence:

Rule 7.1. Positive self-talk: This principle focuses on harnessing your internal dialogue to boost confidence and overcome challenges.

Rule 7.2. Constructive self-reflection: This principle emphasizes turning your inner critic into a supportive coach, learning from every experience.

Rule 7.3. Mental reset techniques: This principle involves developing strategies to maintain a clear, focused mind throughout the game.

Let's consider how these principles could be applied across different sports:

Volleyball

During a tense volleyball match, a referee uses positive self-talk to stay confident when making a close line call (Rule 7.1). After the game, they reflect constructively on their performance, identifying areas for improvement without harsh self-criticism (Rule 7.2). They use a centering breath between points throughout the match to maintain focus and consistency (Rule 7.3).

Field Hockey

A field hockey umpire employs positive self-talk to stay composed during a heated argument with a coach (Rule 7.1). They later reflect on the interaction, considering how to handle similar situations more effectively in the future (Rule 7.2). Throughout the game, they momentarily make physical contact with their whistle, noticing its feel. This technique brings them to the moment, allowing them to approach each new play with a fresh perspective (Rule 7.3).

Swimming

At a swimming competition, an official uses positive self-talk to maintain concentration during long events (Rule 7.1). After each race, they constructively reflect on their timing and coordination with other officials (Rule 7.2). They drink water and briefly stretch between events to stay sharp and focused (Rule 7.3).

In each case, the three principles work together:
- Positive self-talk is the cheerleader
- Constructive self-reflection is the coach
- Mental reset techniques are the reset button

When all three elements align, you create an environment where you maintain confidence and composure even in high-pressure situations, continuously learn and improve from every officiating experience, approach each decision with a clear, focused mind, and enjoy greater resilience and mental endurance throughout long or challenging games.

Remember: Your inner voice is your most powerful officiating tool. Nurture it, listen to it, and let it guide you to excellence.

To implement the learnings from Rule 7 – Your Inner Coach, download your bonus copy of *The Whistle Blower Workbook.*

Scan this QR code or visit: https://books.drjolukins.com/tn2elyoas6

RULE 8

THE BOUNCE-BACK BLUEPRINT

"Toughness isn't just physical; it's the whisper of persistence when all odds stand against you."
—Sandjest

THE ABILITY TO BOUNCE BACK FROM SETBACKS IS CRUCIAL. This rule focuses on developing mental resilience and quick recovery strategies, essential components of mental toughness that allow officials to maintain their effectiveness throughout the game, regardless of challenges.

When setbacks happen—whether it's a missed call, unexpected criticism, or a sudden shift in the game's momentum—how you respond makes all the difference. Mentally resilient officials learn to take mistakes and have strategies to quickly refocus, learn from the moment, and move forward with confidence. This ability to recover swiftly not only preserves your own performance but also sets a strong example for players and coaches, reinforcing your role as a steady, reliable presence on the court.

Within Rule 8, we will explore recovery mechanisms for challenging moments and how they fundamentally impact your officiating performance.

Rule 8.1: Rapid Mental Rebound Technique—Quick Recovery
Rule 8.2: Building Mental Resilience—The Long Game
Rule 8.3: Mental Recovery During Breaks—Recharge and Refocus

This mental rule emphasizes the power of resilience in officiating. Mastering recovery mechanisms enhances your ability to maintain consistent performance throughout the game, ensuring that individual setbacks don't derail one's overall effectiveness as an official.

Resilience is not about avoiding falls, but mastering the art of rising. This rule equips you with the tools to rise stronger after every challenge, transforming potential setbacks into opportunities for growth and improved performance.

RULE 8.1

RAPID MENTAL REBOUND TECHNIQUE— QUICK RECOVERY

The Call

In a high-speed game, mistakes by players and officials are inevitable. What separates great officials from good ones is not their ability to avoid errors but their capacity to recover quickly and maintain their focus. This principle explores how to develop quick recovery strategies, so you can bounce back from setbacks and maintain your effectiveness throughout the game.

Imagine a tennis umpire who makes a disputed call, leading to a heated argument with a player. The ability to quickly reset and refocus is crucial, ensuring the official remains composed and manages the game effectively.

Quick recovery strategies involve developing a post-error routine, learning to reset quickly after mistakes, and creating mental distance from difficult moments. These techniques are essential for maintaining consistency and composure, even in adversity.

The Advantage

Officials who master quick recovery strategies gain several significant benefits. They can maintain their focus and composure even after making a mistake, which helps prevent a single error from cascading into a series of poor decisions. This ability to reset quickly enhances their resilience, allowing them to handle the mental strain of officiating more effectively.

Even in challenging situations, these officials tend to project a sense of calm authority. By quickly overcoming mistakes, they demonstrate to players and coaches that they are in control and capable of effectively managing the game's dynamics. This can increase respect and trust from game participants, who perceive the official as composed and professional.

Another key advantage is improved performance consistency. By learning to reset after mistakes, officials can maintain their high officiating standards throughout the game rather than letting errors affect their confidence or focus.

The Penalty

Officials struggling with quick recovery strategies often face significant challenges that undermine their performance. They may dwell on errors without a reliable method for bouncing back from mistakes, leading to decreased confidence and focus. This can result in a downward spiral, where each mistake compounds the next, affecting their performance and overall mental state.

When officials can't quickly recover, they may appear less composed or authoritative to players and coaches. This perceived lack of control can lead to increased challenges to their decisions and a more difficult game environment overall. In high-pressure situations, the inability to reset quickly can exacerbate stress and anxiety, potentially leading to burnout or decreased performance over time.

The Game Plan

To develop effective quick recovery strategies, focus on creating a simple yet powerful post-error routine. This routine should help you reset your mind and refocus on the game immediately after a mistake.

1. *Develop a consistent mental reset technique.* This might involve taking a few deep breaths, visualizing a successful call, or using a specific phrase to refocus your attention. You can draw on some of the techniques you considered in rule 7.3. Practice this technique regularly so it becomes automatic, allowing you to clear your mind and move forward quickly.

For example, imagine you're a football referee who has just made a disputed penalty call. As soon as the play is over, take a deep breath through your nose and out through your mouth. Visualize yourself making accurate calls, reinforcing your confidence and composure. Then, focus on the next play, using your reset technique to ensure you're fully present and focused.

2. *Create mental distance from difficult moments.* This involves recognizing that mistakes are part of the game and not letting them define your performance. Practice self-compassion by acknowledging the error without dwelling on it. Instead, focus on what you can learn from the situation to improve.

3. *Natural breaks in the game to reset quickly.* During timeouts or between quarters, take a moment to reflect on your performance, identify areas for improvement, and mentally prepare for the next segment of the game. This proactive approach helps you maintain focus and composure, even when facing challenges.

By consistently applying these strategies, you'll develop the ability to recover easily from mistakes, maintaining your effectiveness and composure throughout the game. Quick recovery is not about avoiding errors but how quickly you can regain your focus and continue performing at your best.

As you master this principle, you'll likely find that your officiating becomes more consistent, your confidence grows, and your ability to handle pressure improves. Your quick recovery strategies will become a powerful tool in your officiating toolkit, helping you navigate even the most challenging situations with poise and authority.

RULE 8.2

BUILDING MENTAL RESILIENCE— THE LONG GAME

The Call

Mental resilience is not just an asset—it's a necessity. This principle focuses on developing the mental toughness required to turn setbacks into comebacks, build resilience through challenges, and maintain perspective under fire. It's about cultivating a mindset that views difficulties not as insurmountable obstacles but as opportunities for growth and improvement.

Imagine an ice hockey referee who made a controversial call that led to a heated dispute with a coach. The referee's ability to maintain composure, learn from the experience, and continue officiating at a high level is a testament to mental resilience. This principle is about developing the inner strength that allows officials to weather the storm and emerge stronger and more capable.

Building mental resilience involves reframing setbacks as learning opportunities, actively seeking out challenges to strengthen your officiating skills, and practicing self-forgiveness while maintaining a broader perspective on your role in the game.

The Advantage

Officials who master mental resilience gain a significant edge in their performance and career longevity. They develop the ability to maintain high-performance levels even under intense pressure or after making mistakes. This consistency is highly valued in officiating and can lead to more high-profile assignments and career advancement opportunities.

Mentally resilient officials tend to have a more positive outlook on their role. They see challenges as opportunities to grow rather than threats to their competence. This positive attitude enhances their enjoyment of officiating and contributes to a better game atmosphere for all participants.

Another key advantage is improved decision-making under pressure. Officials with strong mental resilience are less likely to be swayed by external pressures or their own emotions, allowing them to make clearer, more objective decisions even in high-stress situations.

Mental resilience also contributes to long-term career sustainability. Officiating can be a mentally demanding profession, and those who can build and maintain mental toughness are better equipped to handle the rigors of the job over time, reducing the risk of burnout.

The Penalty

Officials who struggle with mental resilience often face significant challenges that can undermine their performance and job satisfaction. They may be more susceptible to stress and anxiety, particularly in high-pressure situations. This can lead to inconsistent performance, with their officiating quality fluctuating based on the game's intensity or recent experiences.

When you lack mental resilience, you may have difficulty overcoming mistakes or criticism. A bad call or negative interaction with a coach or player might affect your confidence for an extended period, potentially impacting your performance in subsequent games.

These officials may also struggle with maintaining perspective, often exaggerating minor setbacks or taking criticism too personally. This can lead to a negative spiral in which each challenge further erodes their confidence and effectiveness.

In the long term, a lack of mental resilience can lead to burnout or early retirement from officiating. The cumulative stress of dealing with challenges without adequate coping mechanisms can make the job feel overwhelming, potentially shortening what could have been a rewarding career.

The Game Plan

To build mental resilience and transform setbacks into opportunities for growth, focus on implementing a structured approach to challenges and self-reflection.

1. *Develop a challenge log.* After each game, record one or two significant challenges you faced. For each challenge, write down:
- What happened
- How you responded
- What you learned
- How you'll apply this lesson in future games

This practice helps reframe difficulties as learning opportunities and builds a record of your growth over time.

2. *Implement the perspective shift technique.* When faced with a setback, ask yourself three questions:
- How important will this seem in a week? A month? A year?
- What can I learn from this situation?
- How can this experience make me a better official?

This approach helps maintain a broader perspective and turns setbacks into opportunities for improvement.

3. Incorporate regular mental toughness training into your preparation routine. This could involve:
- Visualizing yourself handling difficult situations calmly and effectively.
- Practicing deep breathing or other relaxation techniques to use during games.
- Setting small, achievable challenges for yourself in each game (e.g., maintaining perfect positioning for an entire quarter).

4. Develop a quick reset ritual to practice self-forgiveness and maintain perspective under fire. This could be as simple as taking a deep breath, adjusting your cap or whistle, and mentally saying, "Next play." Use this ritual whenever you must let go of a mistake or refocus after a challenging interaction.

Imagine you're a baseball umpire who has just made a controversial call at home plate. The crowd is booing, and the manager is arguing the call. After the interaction, use your reset ritual. Take a deep breath, adjust your mask, and say to yourself, "Next play." Then, in your next break, jot down a quick note about the situation in your challenge log. After the game, reflect on the incident using the perspective shift questions.

Consistently applying these strategies will help you develop greater mental resilience over time. Remember, building mental toughness is a gradual process. Be patient with yourself and celebrate small improvements along the way.

As you master this principle, you'll likely find that you handle challenges with increasing ease and confidence. Your ability to maintain composure under pressure will improve, and you'll start to view difficulties not as threats but as opportunities to showcase and further develop your officiating skills.

Mental resilience is like a muscle—it grows stronger with consistent exercise. By actively engaging with challenges and learning from them, you're not just becoming a better official but developing a valuable life skill that will serve you well both on and off the field.

RULE 8.3

MENTAL RECOVERY DURING BREAKS— RECHARGE AND REFOCUS

THE CALL

In the intense world of sports officiating, breaks in the game are not just physical pauses—they're crucial opportunities to reset and refocus. This principle emphasizes the importance of using these moments effectively to maintain peak performance throughout the game. Whether it's a time-out, a quarter break, or even the brief pauses between plays, each offers a chance to recalibrate your mental state and prepare for the challenges ahead.

Imagine a basketball referee in the final minutes of a close game. Using a time-out to reset mentally, rapidly recover from any emotional strain, and maintain a broader perspective on the game can be the difference between maintaining control and losing it in those crucial moments.

Effective use of breaks involves developing techniques for quick mental resets, practicing rapid emotional recovery, and consistently reminding yourself of the broader context of your role in the game. These skills are essential for maintaining consistency, composure, and effectiveness throughout the contest.

The Advantage

Officials who master the effective use of breaks gain several significant benefits. They often demonstrate remarkable consistency in their performance, maintaining high levels of focus and decision-making quality from the first whistle to the last. This consistency builds trust with players and coaches, who rely on the official's steady presence throughout the game.

A further benefit of using effective breaks is the increase in higher emotional resilience. Using breaks to reset and recover, they can shake off the effects of tense moments or difficult decisions, approaching each new game segment with a fresh mindset. This ability to "wipe the slate clean" can prevent the accumulation of stress and fatigue that might otherwise impact their performance.

Another key advantage is improved situational awareness. When you use the breaks effectively, you often return to the game with a clearer understanding of the overall context, allowing you to anticipate potential issues and manage the game more proactively. This broader perspective can lead to better game management and fewer conflicts.

The Penalty

Officials who struggle to use breaks effectively often face challenges that can undermine their performance. They may carry the emotional baggage of earlier incidents into subsequent parts of the game, potentially clouding their judgment or affecting their interactions with players and coaches. This emotional carryover can lead to inconsistent officiating or escalated tensions on the field.

Without the effective use of breaks, officials may experience increased mental fatigue as the game progresses. This can result in slower reaction times, decreased attention to detail, or poor positioning in crucial late-game situations when clear thinking and quick reactions are most needed.

Officials who don't reset and refocus during breaks may also lose sight of the game's broader context. They might become too focused on individual incidents or interactions, missing important shifts in the contest's dynamics. This tunnel vision can lead to missed calls or inappropriate responses to game situations.

The Game Plan

To master the effective use of breaks and enhance your officiating performance, focus on implementing a structured approach to these crucial moments.

1. Develop a break routine. You can use a break routine consistently during time-outs, quarter breaks, or other pauses in play. This routine should include these key elements:
- Mental reset: Take three deep breaths, focusing on exhaling fully. As you breathe, visualize releasing any tension or residual emotions from the previous play or game segment.
- Refocus: Quickly review your key officiating priorities. Remind yourself of your positioning responsibilities and any specific aspects of the game you need to watch closely.
- Perspective check: Take a moment to consider the broader context of the game. Ask yourself: "What's the score? How much time is left? Are there any brewing tensions I need to be aware of?"
- Smile! You referee because it is a challenge for you and an enjoyable role. Smiling resets your emotional tone and makes relaxing and flowing through the game easier.

Practice this routine until it becomes second nature. This will allow you to complete these steps quickly and effectively, even during short breaks.

2. *The emotional anchor technique for rapid emotional recovery.* Choose a physical object you carry during games—perhaps your whistle or a small item in your pocket. When you feel emotions running high, touch this object and use it as a trigger to remind yourself to stay calm and objective. Over time, this physical action can become a powerful tool for quick emotional resets.

3. *The zooming out habit during longer breaks.* Mentally step back and consider the game as a whole to maintain a broader perspective:
- How has the overall tone of the game evolved?
- Are there any patterns in player behavior or team tactics you need to be aware of?
- How can you best contribute to a fair and well-managed conclusion to the contest?

This broader view can help you make more informed decisions and manage the game more effectively.

Imagine you're refereeing a football (soccer) match. A contentious offside decision led to a disallowed goal, and the scoring team's coach called a time-out to argue the call. As the players gather with their coaches, go through your break routine:
- Take three deep breaths, releasing the tension from the argument.
- Remind yourself of your positioning for the upcoming restart and the need to watch for retaliatory fouls.
- Consider the score, the time left, and the game's overall atmosphere.
- Touch your emotional anchor (perhaps your red card in your pocket) to reset your emotional state.
- Then, take a moment to zoom out, considering how this incident fits into the broader context of the match and how you can best manage the remainder of the game.

By consistently applying these strategies, you'll develop the ability to use breaks effectively, maintaining your focus, composure, and perspective throughout the game. Remember, every break is an opportunity to reset and improve your officiating performance.

As you master this principle, you'll likely find that your energy levels remain more consistent, your decision-making stays sharp (even in late-game situations), and your overall game management improves. Effectively using breaks becomes a powerful tool in your officiating arsenal, helping you navigate even the most challenging contests with skill and composure.

Resilience is not about avoiding falls, but mastering the art of rising. In officiating, this rising happens not just after major setbacks but in the small moments between plays and during breaks. By mastering these moments, you build the resilience to handle the game's challenges.

RULE 8 IN SUMMARY
THE BOUNCE-BACK BLUEPRINT RULE

THINK OF THESE THREE RULES AS PUZZLE PIECES THAT FIT together to equip officials with resilience and recovery strategies to maintain peak performance despite challenges:

Rule 8.1. Rapid mental rebound: Develop a post-error routine to quickly reset after mistakes, creating mental distance from difficult moments, and maintaining composure during adversity.

Rule 8.2. Build mental resilience: Turn setbacks into comebacks, practice self-forgiveness, and maintain perspective under pressure, fostering long-term mental toughness.

Rule 8.3. Recharge and refocus during breaks: Use game breaks effectively for a mental reset, emotional recovery, and gaining a broader perspective to sustain consistent performance throughout the game.

Let's think about how these rules could be applied across different sports:

Tennis

Imagine an umpire who makes a disputed call. They use a post-error routine of taking deep breaths (Rule 8.1) to refocus and maintain composure. They maintain composure and view the dispute as an opportunity to strengthen their resilience (Rule 8.2), and their break routine (Rule 8.3) allows them to reset emotionally and prepare for upcoming challenges.

Ice Hockey

A referee facing criticism for a controversial call mentally distances themselves from the incident and refocuses on the game (Rule 8.1), reframing the setback as a learning opportunity (Rule 8.2). Between periods, they regain perspective and prepare for the next segment of the match (Rule 8.3).

Lacrosse

In the final minutes of a close game, a referee can use a quick recovery strategy (Rule 8.1) to refocus after a tense interaction with players or coaches. They build resilience by reframing challenging situations as learning opportunities (Rule 8.2) helping them focus on their role rather than external pressures. During timeouts, they use the break to reset mentally, helping them approach the remainder of the game with clarity (Rule 8.3).

In each case, the three rules work together:
- Rapid rebound is like a quick reset button that clears mental clutter after mistakes.
- Resilience is like building a shield that transforms setbacks into growth opportunities.

- Game breaks can be like a recharge station, allowing you to restore your focus.

When all three elements align, you create an environment where mistakes are quickly overcome without cascading into larger issues, resilience is strengthened through challenges rather than diminished by them, emotional recovery prevents stress accumulation during games, and performance consistency is maintained from start to finish.

Remember: Resilience is not about avoiding falls, but mastering the art of rising.

To implement the learnings from Rule 8 – The Bounce-Back Blueprint, download your bonus copy of *The Whistle Blower Workbook*.

Scan this QR code or go to visit: https://books.drjolukins.com/tn2elyoas6

RULE 9

PRESSURE POINTS

"Pressure is a privilege."
—Virgil van Dijk

IN THE WORLD OF SPORTS OFFICIATING, PRESSURE IS AN EVER-present companion. This rule focuses on thriving when the heat is on, and the stakes are high, transforming pressure from a potential hindrance into a catalyst for peak performance.

Learning to channel pressure into focused energy starts with mindset. By embracing the intensity of the moment and trusting your preparation, you can stay present, make clear decisions, and even elevate your performance when it matters most. This approach not only helps you manage your own nerves but also inspires confidence in others.

Within Rule 9, we will explore pressure management techniques and how they fundamentally impact your officiating performance, especially in high-stakes situations.

Rule 9.1: Emotional Control—Staying Calm Under Fire
Rule 9.2: Composure Techniques—Keeping Your Cool
Rule 9.3: Pressure as Opportunity—Turning Stress into Strength

This mental rule emphasizes the power of embracing pressure in officiating. By mastering pressure management techniques, you can perform at your best when it matters most, ensuring consistent, high-quality officiating even in the most challenging and high-stakes environments. Pressure doesn't break you; it reveals your true strength.

RULE 9.1

EMOTIONAL CONTROL—STAYING CALM UNDER FIRE

The Call

Emotional control is not just a virtue—it's a necessity. This principle focuses on maintaining a level head and making decisions based on rules and observations rather than emotional reactions. It's about developing the ability to stay neutral in heated moments and recognizing and managing your emotional triggers.

Imagine a crucial moment in a championship game: a potential game-changing call needs to be made, players are shouting, coaches are gesticulating wildly, and the crowd is in an uproar. In this cauldron of emotion, the official who can remain calm and decide based on what they've seen, rather than being swayed by the emotional atmosphere, is the one who truly excels.

Emotional control involves three key elements: understanding how emotions can dictate decisions, staying neutral in heated moments, and recognizing and managing your emotional triggers. These skills are essential for maintaining fairness, consistency, and authority throughout the game.

The Advantage

Officials who master emotional control gain several significant benefits. They can make clearer, more objective decisions, even in high-pressure situations. This consistency in decision-making builds trust with players and coaches, who rely on the official's steady presence regardless of the game's emotional temperature.

Officials with these skills often have a calming effect on the game itself. Their composed demeanor can help de-escalate tense situations, preventing minor disagreements from escalating into major conflicts. This ability to maintain control makes for a smoother game and enhances the official's authority and respect on the field.

Another key advantage is improved focus and mental clarity. By not getting caught up in the emotional swings of the game, you can maintain your concentration on the crucial aspects of play, leading to more accurate calls and better overall game management.

Officials with strong emotional control also tend to enjoy their role more and experience less stress. They're less likely to take criticism personally or let a difficult game affect their mood long after the final whistle.

The Penalty

Officials who struggle with emotional control face several challenges that can undermine their effectiveness. They may make inconsistent calls based on the emotional context rather than the actual infractions, leading to lost credibility with players and coaches. This can result in more arguments and challenges to their authority, making the game harder to manage.

Furthermore, officials who let emotions dictate their decisions may escalate game tensions rather than calm them. A visibly frustrated or angry official can heighten emotions among players and coaches, potentially leading to a loss of control over the game's atmosphere.

These officials may also experience higher levels of stress and burnout. The emotional toll of getting caught up in every heated moment can be exhausting, potentially affecting their performance in a single game and their long-term enjoyment of and commitment to officiating.

Lastly, a lack of emotional control can damage a person's reputation. Officials known for their emotional reactions or inconsistent calls in high-pressure situations may be passed over for important assignments or face increased scrutiny from supervisors and evaluators.

THE GAME PLAN

Focus on implementing a straightforward yet effective strategy to develop strong emotional control and enhance your officiating performance.

1. *Develop an emotional anchor.* This is a quick, discreet action you can perform to center yourself in heated moments. It might be taking a deep breath, touching your whistle, or briefly closing your eyes. Practice using this anchor regularly, even in calm situations, so it becomes second nature when needed.

2. *Stay neutral in heated moments, adopt the mirror technique.* When interacting with an agitated player or coach, consciously mirror calm body language. Speak slowly and quietly, maintain a neutral facial expression, and keep your gestures minimal. This helps you stay composed and can also have a calming effect on others.

3. *For recognizing and managing your emotional triggers, create an emotional inventory.* After each game, jot down:
- Situations that triggered strong emotions
- How you reacted
- How you wish you had reacted

Review this inventory regularly to identify patterns and develop strategies for common triggers.

Imagine you're refereeing a crucial soccer match. A player commits a hard tackle, and as you reach for your card, the offending team's coach starts shouting at you. You feel your anger rising. This is the moment to use your emotional anchor, perhaps touching your wristwatch while taking a deep breath. As you approach the coach, use the mirror technique, speaking calmly and maintaining neutral body language. After the game, add this incident to your emotional inventory, noting how you handled it and any areas for improvement.

Consistently applying these strategies will help you develop stronger emotional control over time. The goal isn't to become emotionless, but to channel your emotions constructively, using them to fuel your focus and energy rather than cloud your judgment.

As you master this principle, you'll likely find that you handle high-pressure situations more easily. Your decisions will become more consistent, your interactions with players and coaches more productive, and your overall enjoyment of officiating will likely increase.

Emotional control is like a muscle—it strengthens with regular exercise. Each game presents new opportunities to practice and improve. Embrace these challenges, knowing that you'll become a more effective, respected, and resilient official with each one.

RULE 9.2

COMPOSURE TECHNIQUES—KEEPING YOUR COOL

The Call

Maintaining composure under pressure is critical when officiating. This principle focuses on developing techniques for keeping your face neutral, body language calm, and emotions channeled into focused energy. These skills are essential for maintaining authority and consistency throughout the game.

Imagine a touch football referee who has just made a crucial call in a semi-final game. The crowd is on its feet, players are arguing, and the coaches are visibly fraught. The official's ability to remain composed, with a neutral expression and calm demeanor, maintains order and respect on the field. It's about projecting confidence and control, even in the most intense moments.

The Advantage

Officials who master composure techniques gain several significant benefits. They often project an aura of calm authority, stabilizing the game environment. This composure helps prevent minor incidents from escalating into major conflicts, as players and coaches are less likely to challenge an official who appears in control.

Officials tend to perform more consistently under pressure when they have skills of composure to utilise. By channeling their emotions into focused energy, they can maintain concentration and make clearer decisions, even in high-stress situations. This ability to stay composed also enhances their ability to manage the game's flow, anticipate potential issues, and respond proactively.

Another key advantage is improved communication with players and coaches. Officials who are calm are more likely to be heard and respected, as their composure lends credibility to their words. This can lead to smoother interactions and fewer confrontations, creating a more positive game atmosphere overall.

The Penalty

Officials struggling with composure techniques often face challenges that undermine their effectiveness. They may appear uncertain or flustered in high-pressure situations, eroding players' and coaches' trust and respect. This perceived lack of control can lead to more frequent challenges to their decisions and a more difficult game environment overall.

Furthermore, officials who can't maintain composure may react impulsively to emotional situations. This can result in inconsistent officiating, as decisions are influenced by the moment rather than objective criteria. Over time, this inconsistency can damage an official's reputation and decrease confidence in their abilities.

These officials may also experience increased stress and fatigue. The emotional toll of struggling to maintain composure can be significant, potentially affecting their performance in a single game and their long-term enjoyment of and commitment to officiating.

THE GAME PLAN

To develop effective composure techniques and enhance your officiating performance, focus on implementing a simple yet powerful approach.

1. *The neutral face technique.* In front of a mirror, practice maintaining a neutral expression while imagining different scenarios that might trigger strong emotions during a game. This could be a disputed call, a confrontation with a coach, or a tense moment with a player. The goal is to develop a "poker face" that doesn't betray your emotions, even when feeling intense pressure.

2. *Body language.* Develop a calm posture routine that you can use during games. This might involve standing straight, relaxing your shoulders, and avoiding fidgeting or aggressive gestures. Practice this posture in low-stakes first, then gradually apply it in more intense games. For more ideas on this, refer to rule 6.2.

3. *Use the breath-to-motion technique to channel emotions into focused energy,* . Whenever you feel emotional, take a deep breath through your nose and out through your mouth. As you exhale, focus on your next action—making a call, moving into position, or communicating with a player. This simple technique helps convert emotional energy into productive action.

Imagine you're refereeing a hockey game, and a player commits a high-sticking penalty. The opposing team's players are upset, and the coach is arguing the call. As you approach the situation, use your neutral face technique to maintain a calm expression. Keep your body language relaxed and composed, avoiding gestures that might escalate tensions. Take a deep breath and focus on the next step—perhaps issuing a penalty or explaining the call to the coach. As you breathe out, channel your energy into the action, ensuring you remain focused and in control.

In this scenario, you might say, "Coach, I understand your concern, but the high stick was clear. I'll explain it to the players." Maintaining calm communication and a composed demeanor can de-escalate the situation and keep the game moving smoothly. If necessary, you could also verbally caution players involved in minor disputes to prevent further escalation.

By consistently applying these strategies, you'll develop greater composure under pressure. Remember, composure is not about suppressing emotions but channeling them into productive energy that enhances your performance.

As you master this principle, you'll likely find that you handle high-pressure situations more easily. Your composure will become a hallmark of your officiating style, earning respect from players, coaches, and fellow officials. Composure is not just a skill—it's a foundation for excellence in officiating, allowing you to perform at your best in any game situation.

RULE 9.3

PRESSURE AS OPPORTUNITY—TURNING STRESS INTO STRENGTH

The Call

In sports officiating, pressure is often viewed as a challenge to overcome. This principle, however, reframes pressure as an opportunity—a chance to showcase your skills, demonstrate your preparation, and rise to the occasion. It's about building confidence from thorough preparation, recognizing that pressure is a privilege reserved for those in important roles, and using controlled breathing to stay centered in high-stress situations.

Imagine a baseball umpire behind home plate in the ninth inning of a no-hitter. The stadium is electric, and every pitch is crucial. At this moment, the official who sees this pressure as an opportunity to demonstrate their expertise rather than a burden to bear is the one who truly excels.

Pressure as an opportunity involves three key elements: building confidence through thorough preparation, remembering that pressure is a privilege, and using controlled breathing techniques to maintain composure. These skills are essential for not just handling pressure but thriving under it.

The Advantage

Officials who master seeing pressure as an opportunity gain several significant benefits. They often perform at their best in high-stakes situations, rising to the occasion rather than shrinking from it. This ability to elevate your game when it matters most can lead to more high-profile assignments and career advancement opportunities.

These officials also tend to enjoy their role more fully. By viewing pressure as a privilege, they find satisfaction in being entrusted with important responsibilities. This positive mindset can lead to greater job satisfaction and longevity.

Another advantage is improved resilience. Officials who embrace pressure are better equipped to handle criticism and setbacks, seeing them as part of the privilege of their role rather than as personal attacks. This resilience allows them to bounce back quickly from difficult games or decisions.

When you see pressure as an opportunity, you inspire confidence in others. Players and coaches can sense when an official is comfortable under pressure, which can have a calming effect on the entire game environment.

The Penalty

Officials who struggle to see pressure as an opportunity face several challenges that can undermine their effectiveness. When faced with high-stakes situations, they may experience anxiety or dread, leading to hesitation or indecision at crucial moments. Players and coaches can perceive this uncertainty, potentially inviting more challenges to their authority.

Furthermore, these officials may try to avoid pressure rather than embrace it. This could lead to a tendency to make "safe" calls rather than correct ones or to shy away from making tough decisions when needed most. Over time, this avoidance can limit an official's growth and career progression.

Officials who view pressure negatively may also experience higher stress levels and burnout. The constant feeling of being under threat rather than rising to a challenge can significantly damage mental health and job satisfaction.

THE GAME PLAN

To develop the ability to see pressure as an opportunity and enhance your officiating performance, focus on implementing the following powerful strategies.

1. *Develop a pressure privilege phrase.* This should be a short, powerful phrase reminding you of the honor of your role. It might be something like "I've earned this moment" or "This is why I officiate." Repeat this phrase to yourself during pre-game preparation and in high-pressure moments during the game.

2. *Box breathing technique:*
- Inhale quietly through your nose for 4 seconds
- Pause your breath for 4 seconds
- Exhale completely through your mouth for 4 seconds
- Pause your breath for 4 seconds

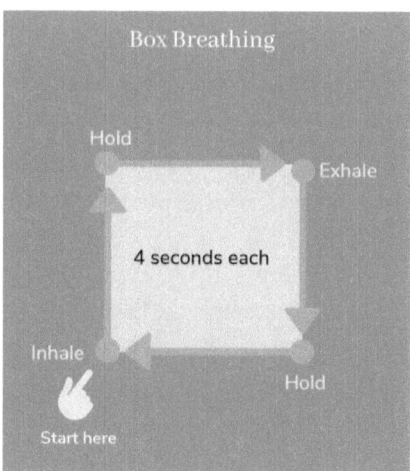

Practice this breathing pattern regularly to employ it during games and maintain composure easily. If you find that 4 seconds is too long and you get dizzy, try a shorter time frame. The key benefit of the strategy is steadying and making your breath consistent.

Imagine you're refereeing a crucial basketball playoff game. As you step onto the court, feeling the crowd's energy, you remind yourself of your pressure privilege phrase: "I've earned this moment." During a tense moment in the fourth quarter, as you prepare to make a crucial call, you use the box breathing technique to center yourself before making your decision.

By consistently applying these strategies, you'll develop the ability to see pressure as an opportunity rather than a threat. Each high-pressure situation is a chance to demonstrate your skills and grow as an official. As you master this principle, you'll likely find that you handle pressure better and thrive on it. Your ability to perform at your best when the stakes are highest will become a hallmark of your officiating style, earning you respect from players, coaches, and fellow officials.

Embracing pressure as opportunity is a mindset that develops over time. Each game, each crucial call, is a chance to reinforce this perspective. Embrace these moments, knowing that with each one, you're not just officiating a game—you're seizing an opportunity to showcase your expertise and contribute to the sport at its highest level.

RULE 9 IN SUMMARY
THE PRESSURE POINTS RULE

THINK OF THESE THREE RULES AS PUZZLE PIECES THAT FIT together to equip officials with strategies to thrive under pressure, transforming them into a catalyst for peak performance:

Rule 9.1. Emotional control under fire: Stay neutral in heated moments and recognize and manage emotional triggers to ensure clear-headed decision-making under intense pressure.

Rule 9.2. Keeping your cool: Maintain a neutral face and calm body language, channel emotions into focused energy, and project confidence and control.

Rule 9.3. Turn stress into strength: View pressure as a privilege, and use controlled breathing techniques to stay centered in high-stress situations.

Let's consider how these rules could be applied across different sports:

College Playoffs

Imagine a referee in a high-stakes playoff game. They use emotional control to remain calm during intense disputes (Rule 9.1), ensuring fair and consistent calls. They maintain composure and project authority (Rule 9.2), preventing minor incidents from escalating. They also see the pressure as an opportunity to showcase their skills, confidently rising to the challenge (Rule 9.3).

Soccer

A referee facing criticism for a controversial call effectively manages their emotions and maintain neutrality (Rule 9.1). They keep calm, which de-escalates tensions and earns respect from players and coaches (Rule 9.2). By viewing the pressure as a privilege (Rule 9.3), they draw confidence from their preparation and stay focused under stress.

Tennis

An umpire in a tense match stays emotionally controlled and makes objective decisions despite the heated atmosphere (Rule 9.1). They maintain composure and neutral body language and channel emotions into productive action (Rule 9.2). They also see the pressure as an opportunity to excel, using controlled breathing to stay centered and perform at their best (Rule 9.3).

In each case, the three rules work together:
- Emotional control is like a shield that protects against triggers
- Keeping calm is like a steady anchor that keeps you grounded
- Seeing pressure as a privilege transforms it into a driving force for excellence

RULE 9 IN SUMMARY

When all three elements align, you create an environment where decisions are made with clarity and consistency. Even in high-pressure situations, officials project confidence and authority, maintaining respect from players and coaches. Pressure is seen as an opportunity for growth and career advancement, and resilience is enhanced, allowing officials to bounce back quickly from setbacks.

Remember: Pressure doesn't break you; it reveals your true strength.

To implement the learnings from Rule 9 – The Pressure Points Rule, download your bonus copy of *The Whistle Blower Workbook*.

Scan this QR code or visit: https://books.drjolukins.com/tn2elyoas6

PART 4
GROWTH AND DEVELOPMENT

THE JOURNEY OF AN OFFICIAL IS ONE OF CONTINUOUS LEARNING and improvement. This final section focuses on the essential elements that contribute to your long-term growth and development in officiating. We'll explore three key rules that will help you evolve from a competent official to an exceptional one, fostering a mindset of lifelong learning and personal growth.

These pages will explore the power of self-reflection, the importance of community support, and the art of thriving in your role. These components are crucial for sustaining your passion for officiating and continually elevating your performance.

Embracing these concepts may require a shift in perspective, but the long-term benefits are immeasurable. Each rule presented here offers strategies to help you become a better official and a more fulfilled individual in your officiating journey.

Rule 10: Reflect and Grow

Learn to continuously harness the power of honest self-evaluation and performance analysis to refine your officiating skills.

Rule 11: Strength in Numbers

Discover the value of creating and nurturing a strong network of fellow officials, mentors, and supporters to enhance your resilience and knowledge.

Rule 12: Thriving in Officiating

Explore techniques to cultivate curiosity, practice gratitude, and maintain a performance mindset. These will ensure your success and help you thrive in your officiating career.

Integrating these rules into your officiating philosophy will create a solid foundation for ongoing growth and fulfillment in your role.

Remember: The most successful officials are not those who know everything, but those who are always eager to learn more.

RULE 10

REFLECT AND GROW

"We do not learn from experience ... we learn from reflecting on experience."
—John Dewey

REFLECTING ON AND LEARNING FROM YOUR PERFORMANCES IS crucial to pursuing officiating excellence. This rule focuses on the systematic debriefing, reviewing, and evolving process through careful performance analysis, transforming each game experience into a stepping stone for improvement.

By making post-game reflection a regular habit, you create opportunities to identify strengths, spot areas for growth, and set clear goals for future improvement. Whether you review game footage, seek feedback from peers, or jot down key moments in a journal, each step helps you gain valuable insights into your decision-making and on-court presence. Over time, this commitment to honest self-assessment not only sharpens your officiating skills but also builds the confidence and adaptability needed to excel in any game situation.

Within Rule 10, we will explore the concept of reflective practice and how it fundamentally impacts your officiating performance and long-term growth.

Rule 10.1: Systematic Self-Evaluation—The Path to Progress
Rule 10.2: Progress Tracking and Celebration—Measuring Success
Rule 10.3: Feedback and Sharing—Learning from Others

This mental rule emphasizes the power of reflection and self-improvement in officiating. By mastering the art of performance analysis and reflective practice, you enhance your ability to learn and grow from every experience, ensuring continuous improvement and increased effectiveness as an official.

This rule equips you with the tools to transform each game, regardless of its outcome, into a valuable learning opportunity, fostering ongoing development, and excellence in your officiating career.

RULE 10.1

SYSTEMATIC SELF-EVALUATION—THE PATH TO PROGRESS

THE CALL

Critical self-analysis is essential for excelling as an official. Regular self-evaluation is key to continuous improvement, enabling you to learn from each game and refine your skills.

This principle focuses on three key elements: recording performance insights immediately after each game, reviewing game film with a clear purpose, and identifying patterns in your decision-making process.

Imagine a volleyball referee who has just finished officiating a challenging match. Instead of simply moving on to the next game, they take the time to reflect on their performance, jot down key observations, and later review the game footage to gain deeper insights. This systematic approach to self-evaluation is what separates good officials from great ones.

The Advantage

Officials who master systematic self-evaluation gain several significant benefits. They experience accelerated skill development, constantly learning from their experiences and applying those lessons to future games. This continuous improvement cycle leads to more consistent and accurate officiating over time.

These officials tend to have a clearer understanding of their strengths and areas for improvement. This self-awareness allows them to focus their training efforts more effectively, leading to more efficient skill enhancement. As officials become more aware of their capabilities and growth, this awareness also increases their confidence.

Another key advantage is identifying and correcting recurring issues before they become ingrained habits. By regularly reviewing their performance and identifying patterns, officials can prevent potential problems and reinforce positive behaviors.

Perhaps most importantly, officials who engage in systematic self-evaluation demonstrate a commitment to excellence that supervisors and peers often recognize. This dedication can lead to more opportunities for high-profile assignments and career advancement.

The Penalty

Officials who neglect systematic self-evaluation face challenges that can hinder their growth and effectiveness. They may repeat the same mistakes game after game, unaware of patterns in their decision-making that need correction. This lack of improvement can lead to stagnation in their officiating careers.

These officials may also struggle with inconsistency in their performance, as they do not actively identify and address areas of weakness. This inconsistency can erode players' and coaches' trust, potentially leading to more on-field conflicts and challenges to their authority.

Without a systematic approach to self-evaluation, officials may also miss opportunities for growth and development. They might overlook subtle aspects of their performance that could be refined or fail to recognize emerging strengths that could be further developed.

Lastly, officials who don't engage in self-evaluation may find handling feedback from supervisors or peers more difficult. Without a habit of self-reflection, external criticism can feel more personal and challenging to incorporate constructively.

The Game Plan

To develop effective systematic self-evaluation skills and enhance your officiating performance, focus on implementing the following strategies.

1. *Create a post-game reflection routine.* This should be a simple process you can complete within 15-30 minutes of every game you officiate.

Here's a basic structure:

Quick debrief (5 minutes):

    Write down three things you did well

    Note 3 areas for improvement

    Record any unusual or challenging situations you encountered

Performance rating (2 minutes):

    Rate your overall performance on a scale of 1-10

    Briefly explain your rating

Key learnings (3 minutes):

    Write down the most important lesson from this game

Make this routine a non-negotiable part of your officiating practice. The goal is to capture your immediate thoughts and feelings while the game is still fresh in your mind.

2. *Implement a game video review session within 48 hours of each game.* If you don't have access to game film for every match, aim to review footage at least once a month. During this session:
- Watch the full game or key segments
- Focus on your positioning, mechanics, and decision-making
- Compare your real-time decisions with what you see on film
- Note any discrepancies or insights

As you review multiple games over time, start looking for patterns in your decision-making. Are there certain types of calls you tend to miss? Do you handle some situations more effectively than others? Keep a running list of these patterns to inform your training focus.

Let's say you're a touch football referee. After a game, you complete your post-game reflection routine. You note that you handled a coach's complaint well (positive) but missed a forward pass in a crucial moment (area for improvement). You rate your performance a 7/10 and write that your key learning was maintaining focus in high-pressure moments.

Two days later, during your game video review session, you watch the missed traveling call. You noticed that your positioning was slightly off, contributing to the missed call. You add "refine positioning for better angle" to your list of focus areas.

Over time, as you review multiple games, you notice a pattern: you tend to miss more calls in the fourth quarter. This insight leads you to develop strategies for maintaining focus late in games.

If you don't receive a video of your games (and at local competitions, you may not), see if you can have a friend or another referee video the game. (Important note: make sure the sporting association approves this. Some games, particularly junior games, may not be allowed to be videoed.)

By consistently applying this systematic self-evaluation approach, you'll develop a deeper understanding of your officiating style, strengths, and areas for improvement. The goal isn't to be overly critical but to create a positive cycle of continuous learning and improvement.

As you master this principle, you'll likely find that your rate of improvement accelerates. Your ability to learn from every game, regardless of its outcome, will become a hallmark of your officiating approach. This commitment to self-evaluation and growth will enhance your performance and contribute to a more fulfilling and successful officiating career.

Systematic self-evaluation is a skill that improves with practice. Embrace each game as an opportunity to learn and grow, knowing each reflection will make you a more insightful, effective, and accomplished official.

RULE 10.2

PROGRESS TRACKING AND CELEBRATION—MEASURING SUCCESS

The Call

Tracking progress and celebrating successes are essential to maintaining motivation and focus in the journey to officiating excellence. This principle focuses on documenting areas for improvement, monitoring progress systematically, and celebrating successes, no matter how small. It's about cultivating a mindset that values growth and acknowledges achievements.

Imagine a tennis umpire who keeps a detailed log of their performance after each match. They note areas where they excelled and need improvement, tracking their progress over time. This systematic approach helps them refine their skills and provides a sense of accomplishment and motivation to continue improving.

Progress tracking and celebration involve three key elements: documenting areas for improvement, tracking progress systematically, and celebrating successes. These practices are crucial for maintaining a positive outlook and reinforcing the behaviors that lead to excellence in officiating.

The Advantage

Officials who master progress tracking and celebration gain several significant benefits. They often experience increased motivation and engagement in their officiating career. By documenting areas for improvement and monitoring progress, they can see tangible evidence of their growth over time, which can be a powerful motivator.

These officials also tend to maintain a more positive mindset. Celebrating successes, even small ones, helps them stay focused on their progress rather than getting discouraged by setbacks or areas for improvement. This positive outlook can lead to greater job satisfaction and enjoyment of the officiating role.

Another key advantage is improved resilience. Officials can better handle criticism or difficult games by acknowledging and celebrating their achievements. They're more likely to view challenges as opportunities for growth rather than threats to their ego or performance.

When you track progress and celebrate successes, you often demonstrate greater self-awareness and self-confidence. You're more likely to recognize your strengths and weaknesses, which allows you to approach challenges with a clearer understanding of your capabilities.

The Penalty

Officials who neglect progress tracking and celebration may struggle with feeling stagnant or unfulfilled in their officiating career as they lack a clear sense of progress or achievement. This can lead to decreased motivation and potentially even burnout.

Without systematic tracking, these officials may miss opportunities to reinforce positive behaviors and correct negative ones. They might not recognize patterns of improvement or areas where they need more focus, leading to inconsistent performance over time.

These officials may also find it harder to maintain a positive mindset. Without celebrating successes, they might focus more on setbacks or criticisms, which can erode their confidence and enjoyment of officiating. Failing to track your progress may see you struggle to set realistic goals or measure effectiveness. This lack of clear direction can lead to frustration and career drift.

The Game Plan

The following strategies will help you develop effective progress tracking to enhance your officiating performance:

1. *Create a progress journal.* This should be a dedicated notebook or digital document where you record your performance insights after each game. Include:
- Areas for improvement: Note specific aspects of your officiating that need work.
- Progress tracking: Set specific, measurable goals for improvement and track your progress over time.
- Successes: Celebrate any achievements, no matter how small they seem.

    For example, after a game, you might write:
    - Area for improvement: Better positioning on corner kicks.
    - Progress: Successfully managed two corner kicks without issues.
    - Success: Handled a difficult coach interaction professionally.

2. *Implement a celebration ritual.* This could be as simple as treating yourself to a favorite meal after a game where you met one of your goals or sharing your successes with a colleague or mentor. The goal is to create a consistent way to acknowledge and celebrate your achievements.

3. *Use a goal-setting template.* At the start of each month or season, set three specific goals related to your officiating performance. These might include improving your reaction time, enhancing your communication with players, or refining your decision-making on particular types of calls. Track your progress towards these goals regularly, adjusting them as needed based on your reflections.

Imagine you're a soccer referee aiming to improve your corner-kick positioning. You set a goal to correctly manage at least 80% of corner kicks without issues over the next five games. After each match, you update your progress journal with your success rate and note any challenges or successes. When you reach your goal, you celebrate by sharing your achievement with a fellow official and treating yourself to a favorite meal.

You'll develop a more positive and growth-oriented mindset by consistently applying these strategies. Progress tracking and celebration are not just about recognizing achievements; they're about creating a culture of continuous improvement and motivation.

As you master this principle, you'll likely find your officiating career more fulfilling. Your ability to track progress and celebrate successes will enhance your performance and contribute to a more positive and resilient mindset, helping you navigate the challenges of officiating with greater ease and confidence.

Progress tracking and celebration are skills that improve with practice. Each game and reflection is an opportunity to reinforce positive behaviors and acknowledge your growth. Embrace this process, knowing you're becoming a more effective, motivated, and accomplished official with each step.

RULE 10.3

FEEDBACK AND SHARING—LEARNING FROM OTHERS

The Call

In sports officiating, continuous improvement is not a solitary journey. This principle focuses on the vital role of feedback and sharing in an official's growth and development. It emphasizes gracefully accepting feedback, sharing lessons with trusted colleagues, and contributing to the wider officiating community. By embracing these practices, officials can accelerate their learning, broaden their perspectives, and contribute to elevating the profession.

Imagine a baseball umpire who, after a challenging game, seeks feedback from their crew chief, openly discusses their experiences with fellow umpires, and later shares their insights at a local officiating clinic. This open approach to feedback and sharing enhances their skills and contributes to the officiating community's collective knowledge.

Feedback and sharing involve three key elements: gracefully accepting input from others, sharing personal learnings with trusted colleagues, and actively contributing to the broader officiating community. These practices are essential for fostering a culture of continuous improvement and mutual support among officials.

The Advantage

Officials who master the art of feedback and sharing often experience accelerated growth in their skills and understanding of the game. By being open to feedback and actively seeking it, they gain valuable insights that might take years to acquire through personal experience alone.

Such officials tend to develop stronger professional networks. By sharing their learnings and engaging with colleagues, they build relationships that provide support, opportunities, and diverse perspectives throughout their careers.

Increased adaptability is another key advantage. When you regularly engage in feedback and sharing you are more likely to stay current with evolving rules, techniques, and best practices in officiating. This adaptability can lead to more consistent and effective performance over time.

Perhaps most importantly, officials who embrace feedback and sharing often find greater fulfillment in their roles. By contributing to the officiating community, they derive a sense of purpose beyond individual games, seeing themselves as part of a larger professional community dedicated to excellence.

The Penalty

Officials who neglect feedback and sharing may face challenges that hinder their growth and effectiveness. They might miss valuable insights and perspectives that could enhance their performance, potentially leading to slower skill development or the persistence of bad habits.

They may also find themselves isolated within the officiating community. Without actively engaging in sharing and feedback, they might lack the support network that can be crucial for navigating challenges and advancing in their careers.

Officials resistant to feedback may also develop a reputation for being difficult to work with or unwilling to improve. This can lead to fewer opportunities for high-profile assignments or leadership roles within officiating organizations.

Lastly, by not contributing to the broader officiating community, these officials miss out on the personal growth and satisfaction that come from mentoring others and contributing to the advancement of the profession.

The Game Plan

The following strategies will help you develop effective feedback and sharing practices to enhance your officiating performance.

1. *Adopt a feedback mindset.* After each game, actively seek feedback from at least one source. This could be your officiating partners, a mentor or supervisor, or self-reflection through video review
When receiving feedback, practice the *Three A's*:
Acknowledge: Thank the person for their input
Ask: Seek clarification or examples if needed
Act: Determine one specific action you'll take based on the feedback if you agree

2. *Implement or attend a group catch-up of trusted officials.* Identify 2-3 trusted colleagues with whom you can regularly exchange experiences and insights. Set up a monthly call or meeting where each person shares:
- A challenge they faced and how they handled it
- A success story and what led to the positive outcome
- A question or area where they're seeking advice

3. *Commit to a give-back goal to contribute to the broader officiating community.* This could be:
   - Volunteering to mentor a new official
   - Offering to present at a local officiating clinic
   - Writing an article for an officiating newsletter or website

Set a specific target, such as mentoring one new official per season or giving one presentation yearly.

Imagine you're a touch football referee working on improving your field positioning. After a game, you ask your referee coach for feedback on your positioning. They suggest you could anticipate play development better. You acknowledge their input, ask for specific examples, and decide to focus on this in your next game.

In your next group catchup, you discuss this feedback and how you're working on it. A colleague shares a visualization technique they use for anticipating the play, which you decide to try.

For your give back goal, you offer to lead a session on court positioning at the next local referee clinic, sharing what you've learned and the techniques you've developed.

You'll create a virtuous learning, sharing, and growth cycle by consistently applying these strategies. Regular reflection turns experience into expertise, and this reflection is enriched through feedback and sharing.

As you master this principle, your officiating career will likely become more dynamic and rewarding. Your openness to feedback, willingness to share, and contributions to the community will enhance your performance and elevate officiating standards.

Each interaction, each shared insight, is an opportunity to learn and grow. Embrace this collaborative approach to improvement, knowing that with each exchange, you're becoming a more knowledgeable, connected, and influential member of the officiating community.

RULE 10 IN SUMMARY
THE REFLECT AND GROW RULE

THINK OF THESE THREE RULES AS PUZZLE PIECES THAT FIT together to help officials continuously improve their performance through structured self-reflection and progress tracking:

Rule 10.1. Systematic self-evaluation: Focuses on recording performance insights immediately after each game, reviewing game footage with a clear purpose, and identifying patterns in decision-making to refine officiating skills.

Rule 10.2. Progress tracking: Teaches you to document areas for improvement, track progress systematically, and celebrate successes to maintain motivation and focus on growth.

Rule 10.3. Feedback and sharing: Encourages officials to seek feedback from trusted sources, share learnings with colleagues, and contribute to the broader officiating community for collective growth.

Let's think about how these rules could be applied across different sports:

Volleyball

A referee completes their post-game reflection routine, noting key observations from challenging matches (Rule 10.1). They track progress on improving their positioning during plays (Rule 10.2) and share insights with fellow referees during a monthly catch-up session (Rule 10.3).

Touch Football

After a game, an official reviews footage to identify missed calls and recurring patterns (Rule 10.1). They set a goal to refine their positioning over the next few matches (Rule 10.2) and seek feedback from a mentor on strategies to improve (Rule 10.3).

Tennis

An umpire reflects on their handling of player disputes after a match (Rule 10.1), celebrates small successes like maintaining composure during tense moments (Rule 10.2), and contributes by sharing their techniques at an officiating clinic (Rule 10.3).

In each case, the three rules work together:
- Self-evaluation acts like a mirror
- Progress tracking is your roadmap
- Feedback and sharing is a community hub

When all three elements align, you create an environment where officials gain deeper self-awareness and accelerate skill development. Progress is tracked systematically, reinforcing positive behaviors and addressing weaknesses, while feedback enriches learning and strengthens professional networks, fostering a culture of continuous improvement leading to greater career satisfaction and advancement.

Remember: Every game is an opportunity to learn, grow, and refine your craft.

To implement the learnings from Rule 10 – Feedback and Sharing – Learning from Others Rule, download your bonus copy of *The Whistle Blower Workbook.*

Scan this QR code or visit: https://books.drjolukins.com/tn2elyoas6

RULE 11

STRENGTH IN NUMBERS

"Having fellow refs around you gives you great opportunities to develop. It will make you a better referee."
—Carol Anne Chenard

BUILDING A STRONG SUPPORT NETWORK IS CRUCIAL FOR developing mental resilience in officiating. This rule focuses on the power of community in enhancing an official's ability to handle challenges, learn from others, and contribute to the profession's growth.

Connecting with other officials provides a valuable source of encouragement, perspective, and practical advice. Sharing experiences—both successes and setbacks—helps normalize the challenges of officiating and reminds you that you're not alone in facing them. Whether through formal mentoring, peer discussions, or online communities, these relationships offer fresh insights, boost confidence, and foster a sense of belonging. Over time, being part of a supportive network not only strengthens your resilience but also furthers your commitment to personal and professional growth within the officiating community.

Within Rule 11, we will explore the concept of building referee networks and how it fundamentally impacts your officiating performance and mental toughness.

Rule 11.1: Building Relationships—The Power of Community
Rule 11.2: Mentorship and Learning—Passing on Wisdom
Rule 11.3: Community Support—Standing Together

This mental rule emphasizes the power of community in officiating. By mastering the art of building and leveraging referee networks, you enhance your resilience and access to knowledge, ensuring a more supported and successful officiating career.

Remember, in unity, we find not just support but amplified strength. This rule equips you with the tools to build a strong support network, transforming your officiating journey from a solitary pursuit into a collective endeavor of growth and excellence.

RULE 11.1

BUILDING RELATIONSHIPS—THE POWER OF COMMUNITY

THE CALL

In sports officiating, the strength of your network can be as crucial as your technical skills. This principle focuses on building meaningful relationships with fellow officials, actively participating in officiating communities, and networking professionally and purposefully. It's about creating a support system that enhances your officiating career and contributes to personal growth and resilience.

Imagine a football referee who, beyond their on-field duties, regularly attends local officiating meetings, participates in online forums for officials, and tries to connect with colleagues at tournaments. This official is not just improving their skills; they're building a network that can provide support, opportunities, and valuable insights throughout their career.

Relationship building in officiating involves three key elements: fostering connections with fellow officials, engaging actively in officiating communities, and approaching networking with a clear purpose and professional mindset. These practices are essential for creating a robust support system to help you navigate officiating challenges and accelerate your professional growth.

The Advantage

Officials who master the art of relationship building often have many resources to draw upon when facing challenges or seeking advice. This network can provide emotional support during tough times, technical insights for improving performance, and even career opportunities as they become known and respected within the officiating community.

Staying more engaged and motivated in their roles is a further benefit. Regular interaction with peers can reignite the passion for officiating, provide fresh perspectives, and help officials remain current with evolving aspects of the game. This engagement often translates to improved on-field performance and job satisfaction.

Another key advantage is the development of a broader perspective on officiating. Through relationships with diverse colleagues, you can learn about different approaches to game management, conflict resolution, and professional development. This expanded viewpoint can enhance decision-making and adaptability in various officiating scenarios.

Strong relationships within the officiating community can create a sense of belonging and purpose beyond individual games or seasons. This sense of community can be a powerful motivator and source of resilience throughout your officiating career.

The Penalty

Officials who neglect relationship building might find themselves isolated within the officiating world, lacking the support and insights gained from a strong network. This isolation can lead to slower skill development, as they miss out on their peers' collective wisdom and experiences.

They may also struggle more with the mental and emotional challenges of officiating. Without a support system to turn to during difficult times, they might find it harder to bounce back from tough games or handle the pressure of high-stakes situations.

When you don't actively build relationships, you may also miss out on career advancement opportunities. Many assignments and promotions in officiating come through connections and recommendations. Without a strong network, you might find your career progression stalling.

By not engaging in the broader officiating community, you risk developing a narrower perspective on your role. This can lead to inflexibility in your approach to officiating and difficulty adapting to new challenges or changes in the game.

THE GAME PLAN

To develop effective relationship-building skills and enhance your officiating network, focus on implementing the following strategies.

1. Create a connection calendar
Set a goal to make one meaningful connection within the officiating community each month. This could involve:
- Reaching out to a colleague you respect for a coffee or video chat
- Attending a local officiating meeting or workshop
- Participating in an online forum or social media group for officials

To make these interactions purposeful, prepare a few questions or topics you'd like to discuss. This preparation ensures that each connection is meaningful and contributes to your growth.

2. The three-tier networking strategy
-Local: Engage with officials in your immediate area or league
-Regional: Expand your network to include officials from neighboring areas or higher-level leagues
-National/international: Connect with officials from different parts of the country or world through online platforms or conferences

Set specific goals for each tier. For example, aim to know all of or most of the officials in your local league, attend one regional officiating event per year, and join an international officiating forum online.

3. *Commit to a community contribution plan*
The plan will lead you to participate more actively in officiating communities. Choose one way you can contribute your time or expertise each season. This might include:
- Volunteering to help organize a local officiating clinic
- Sharing your experiences or insights in an officiating newsletter or blog
- Offering to mentor a new official

Imagine you're a basketball referee looking to expand your network. You start by contacting a respected senior official in your area for coffee. During your meeting, you ask about their career path and any advice they have for advancing in officiating. This connection provides valuable insights and opens doors for future opportunities.

For your regional networking, you decide to attend a state-level officiating conference. Here, you meet officials from different parts of the state and learn about varying approaches to game management. You exchange contact information with several colleagues, expanding your support network.

On the national level, you join an online forum for basketball officials. You commit to posting or commenting at least once a week, sharing your experiences, and learning from others nationwide.

For your community contribution plan, you volunteer to lead a session on court positioning at the next local referee clinic, sharing what you've learned from your expanded network.

You'll build a robust network that supports your growth by consistently applying these strategies. Remember, relationship building is an ongoing process. Each interaction is an opportunity to learn, share, and strengthen your connection to the officiating community.

As you master this principle, you'll likely find your officiating career more rewarding and resilient. Your network will become a source of support, knowledge, and opportunities, enhancing your field performance and overall experience as an official.

Relationship building in officiating is about creating a community that uplifts and supports each member. Embrace this collaborative approach, knowing that with each connection, you're not just improving your officiating journey but contributing to the strength and quality of the officiating community.

RULE 11.2

MENTORSHIP AND LEARNING—PASSING ON WISDOM

The Call

Mentorship is a powerful tool for growth and development in sports officiating. This principle focuses on the dual aspects of mentoring new officials and accepting mentorship from veterans. It emphasizes the importance of sharing experiences and learning from others, fostering a culture of continuous improvement and knowledge transfer within the officiating community.

Imagine a seasoned football referee who mentors a new official and seeks guidance from a veteran colleague. This approach helps the new official develop their skills and allows the seasoned referee to refine their own techniques and stay current with best practices.

Mentorship and learning involve three key elements: mentoring new officials, accepting veteran mentorship, and sharing experiences to learn from others. These practices are essential for creating a supportive environment promoting officials' skill development and resilience.

The Advantage

Officials who master the art of mentorship and learning often experience accelerated skill development, as they can learn from the experiences and insights of others. This can lead to more consistent, accurate officiating and confidence in their abilities.

These officials also tend to develop stronger professional networks. By mentoring and being mentored, they build relationships that can provide support, opportunities, and valuable feedback throughout their careers.

Another advantage is improved adaptability. Officials who engage in mentorship and learning are more likely to stay current with evolving rules, techniques, and best practices in officiating. This adaptability can lead to better performance in high-pressure situations and a greater ability to handle unexpected challenges.

In addition, when you embrace mentorship and learning, you often demonstrate greater resilience and job satisfaction. Being part of a supportive network equips you to handle the mental and emotional demands of officiating, leading to a more fulfilling and sustainable career.

The Penalty

Officials who neglect mentorship and learning may face several challenges that can hinder their growth and effectiveness. They might miss out on valuable insights and experiences that could enhance their performance, potentially leading to slower skill development or the persistence of bad habits.

They may also struggle with isolation within the officiating community. Without engaging in mentorship, they might lack the support and guidance to help them navigate challenges or address areas for improvement.

Officials who don't seek mentorship may also be less adaptable to changes in the game or officiating standards. This inflexibility can decrease performance, as they may fail to incorporate new techniques or perspectives into officiating.

Lastly, by not engaging in mentorship and learning, these officials may miss out on opportunities for personal growth and career advancement. Mentorship relationships can lead to new assignments, promotions, or leadership roles within officiating organizations.

The Game Plan

To develop your mentorship and learning skills, focus on implementing the following powerful approach.

1. Create a mentorship framework.
This involves identifying two key roles:
Mentor: Find a veteran official who can guide you. Set up regular check-ins to discuss your progress, challenges, and goals.
Mentee: Offer to mentor a new official. Share your experiences, provide feedback, and help them set goals for improvement.

For example, you might meet with your mentor monthly to review your performance and discuss strategies for improvement. You might also set up bi-weekly calls with your mentee to review game footage and provide feedback on their officiating.

2. Implement the experience sharing cycle. Regularly share your experiences with fellow officials through informal discussions or more formal presentations at officiating clinics. This could involve:
- Discussing challenging situations and how you handled them
- Sharing tips for improving specific skills
- Reflecting on what you've learned from recent games or training sessions

Commit to a monthly share practice to make this sharing more systematic. Each month, write down one key lesson or insight you've gained from your officiating experiences. Share this with your mentor, mentee, or other officials through a newsletter or online forum.

Imagine you're a basketball referee who has just mentored a new official through their first season. You reflect on the challenges they faced and the strategies that worked well. You share these insights at a local officiating clinic, highlighting the importance of clear communication and proactive game management.

In return, you seek guidance from a veteran referee with high-level tournament experience. You meet with them regularly to discuss your goals and receive feedback on your performance.

You'll develop a strong foundation for continuous learning and growth by consistently applying these strategies. Remember, mentorship is a two-way street—giving and receiving guidance can enrich your officiating journey. As you master this principle, your officiating career will likely become more fulfilling and dynamic. Your ability to learn from others and share your experiences will enhance your performance and contribute to a more supportive and collaborative officiating community.

Mentorship and learning are skills that improve with practice. Each interaction, each shared insight, is an opportunity to grow and refine your officiating skills. Embrace this collaborative approach, knowing that with each mentorship relationship, you're not just improving your officiating journey but contributing to the strength and quality of the officiating community.

RULE 11.3

COMMUNITY SUPPORT—STANDING TOGETHER

The Call

Community support is not just a nicety in sports officiating—it's a necessity. This principle focuses on supporting colleagues through challenges, contributing to the growth of the officiating community, and finding strength in collective experiences. It's about recognizing that officiating is not a solitary pursuit but a shared endeavor where unity and mutual support can amplify individual strengths.

Imagine a soccer referee who, after a tough game, asks a colleague for advice on handling similar situations in the future. This act of support helps the individual and reinforces the bonds within the officiating community, creating a network of mutual aid and encouragement.

Community support involves three key elements: supporting colleagues through challenges, contributing to the growth of the officiating community, and finding strength in collective experiences. These practices are essential for fostering a culture of resilience and collaboration among officials.

The Advantage

Officials who master community support often experience increased resilience and job satisfaction, knowing they can rely on their colleagues for support during difficult times. This sense of belonging to a supportive community can enhance their well-being and motivation.

Community-oriented officials contribute to a more positive and collaborative officiating environment. By actively supporting their peers and contributing to community growth, they help create a culture where officials feel valued and encouraged to improve.

Another key advantage is improved collective knowledge and skill development. When officials support each other and share experiences, they can learn from broader perspectives and insights, leading to more informed decision-making and better overall performance.

Perhaps most importantly, officials who engage in community support often find that their efforts are recognized and valued by peers and supervisors. This recognition can increase respect within the officiating community and potentially create more opportunities for leadership roles or high-profile assignments.

The Penalty

Officials who neglect community support might feel isolated or unsupported within the officiating community, leading to increased stress and decreased resilience during challenging times.

These officials may miss out on opportunities for growth and development. Without engaging in collective learning and support, they may not benefit from their peers' diverse experiences and insights, potentially leading to slower skill development or a lack of adaptability in officiating.

When you don't contribute to the community you may struggle with a sense of purpose or fulfillment. You might also feel disconnected from the broader goals of the officiating community if you don't collaborate to improve officiating standards.

By not finding strength in collective experiences, officials may overlook the power of unity in officiating. This can lead to a more individualistic approach, where challenges are faced alone rather than as part of a supportive team.

The Game Plan

The following strategies will help you develop effective community support skills and enhance your officiating performance:

1. *Create a support network map.* Identify at least three colleagues you can turn to for support or advice. This might include:
- A mentor or experienced official
- A peer who officiates at a similar level
- A colleague from a different officiating background or sport

Regularly check in with these individuals, offering support when needed and seeking advice when facing challenges.

2. *Implement a community contribution plan.* Commit to one specific way you'll contribute to the growth of the officiating community each season. This could be:
- Volunteering to help organize a local officiating clinic
- Writing an article for an officiating newsletter or blog
- Participating in a mentorship program for new officials

Set clear goals for your contribution and track your progress throughout the season.

3. *Adopt the shared reflection practice.* After each game or significant officiating event, take a few minutes to reflect on what you learned

and how you can apply those lessons in the future. Share these reflections with your support network through a group chat, email, or in-person discussion.

Imagine you're a basketball referee who has just officiated a challenging game. You reach out to a colleague from your support network map to discuss the tough calls you made and seek advice on handling similar situations in the future.

You decide to volunteer at a local officiating clinic for your community contribution plan. You lead a session on conflict resolution, sharing your experiences and insights with new officials.

In your shared reflection practice, you write down three key takeaways from the game and share them with your support network. You ask for feedback and suggestions on improving and reinforcing the bonds within your community and gaining valuable insights for future games.

By consistently applying these strategies, you'll develop a strong sense of community support and contribute to a more collaborative officiating environment. This principle equips you with the tools to build a network that supports you and amplifies your abilities as an official.

As you master this principle, you'll likely find your officiating career more fulfilling and resilient. Your ability to support and be supported by your colleagues will enhance your performance and contribute to a more positive and collaborative officiating community.

Embrace this collaborative approach, knowing that with each act of support, you're not just improving your officiating journey but contributing to the strength and quality of the officiating community.

RULE 11 IN SUMMARY
THE STRENGTH IN NUMBERS RULE

THINK OF THESE THREE RULES AS PUZZLE PIECES THAT FIT together to build strong referee networks that enhance mental resilience, foster collaboration, and accelerate growth in officiating:

Rule 11.1. Building Relationships: Focuses on creating meaningful connections with fellow officials, actively participating in officiating communities, and networking professionally to build a robust support system.

Rule 11.2. Mentorship and Learning: Encourages mentoring new officials while seeking guidance from veterans, fostering a culture of shared experiences, continuous improvement, and knowledge transfer.

Rule 11.3. Community Support: Emphasizes supporting colleagues through challenges, contributing to the growth of the officiating community, and finding strength in collective experiences.

Let's consider how these rules could be applied across different sports:

Soccer

A referee builds relationships by attending local officiating meetings (Rule 11.1), mentors a new official while seeking advice from a veteran colleague (Rule 11.2), and shares reflections on game management strategies with peers after matches (Rule 11.3).

Athletics

An official connects with colleagues at regional tournaments (Rule 11.1), participates in a mentorship program to guide newer officials while learning from senior officials (Rule 11.2), and contributes to an officiating clinic by leading a session on conflict resolution (Rule 11.3).

Touch Football

An official engages with their league's community through online forums (Rule 11.1), mentors rookies while gaining insights from experienced referees (Rule 11.2), and volunteers to organize a local workshop on positioning techniques (Rule 11.3).

In each case, the three rules work together:
- Building relationships helps you grow
- Mentorship plants seeds of knowledge
- Community support fosters strength

When all three elements align, you create an environment where officials feel supported and connected within their community, knowledge is shared freely, skill development is accelerated across all levels of officiating, resilience is enhanced through collective experiences and mutual encouragement, and a culture of collaboration leads to greater satisfaction and career advancement.

Remember: In unity, we find not just support, but amplified strength.

To implement the learnings from Rule 11 – The Strength in Numbers Rule – Learning from Others Rule, download your bonus copy of *The Whistle Blower Workbook.*

Scan this QR code or visit: https://books.drjolukins.com/tn2elyoas6

RULE 12

THRIVING IN OFFICIATING

"It's what you learn after you think you know it all that really counts."
—John Wooden

IN THE DEMANDING WORLD OF SPORTS OFFICIATING, MERELY surviving isn't enough. This rule focuses on developing the mindset and practices that allow officials to truly thrive in their roles, embracing challenges as opportunities for growth and finding fulfillment in their service to the game.

When officials shift their focus from simply getting through each game to actively seeking out ways to grow, the experience becomes far more rewarding. Thriving means staying curious, setting personal goals, and celebrating progress—no matter how small. It's about finding purpose in every challenge, learning from setbacks, and taking pride in the positive impact you have on the sport. By adopting this proactive approach, officials not only enhance their own satisfaction and performance but also inspire those around them to pursue excellence and enjoy the journey.

Within Rule 12, we will explore how thriving in officiating fundamentally impacts your performance and overall well-being.

Rule 12.1: Cultivating Curiosity—The Mind of a Learner
Rule 12.2: Practicing Gratitude—Finding Positivity
Rule 12.3: Continuous Learning and Growth—The Journey Never Ends
Bonus Rule: Holistic Well-being—Balancing Life and Sport

This mental rule emphasizes the importance of not just surviving, but thriving in officiating. Mastering these principles enhances your ability to find fulfillment, grow continuously, and maintain well-being, ensuring a long, successful, and satisfying career.

This rule equips you with the tools to transform the pressures of officiating into opportunities for personal and professional growth, allowing you to excel while maintaining a balanced and fulfilling life.

RULE 12.1

CULTIVATING CURIOSITY—THE MIND OF A LEARNER

The Call

In sports officiating, curiosity is a necessity. This principle focuses on developing and maintaining an inquisitive mindset that drives continuous improvement and adaptability. It's about questioning assumptions, delving deeply into rule interpretations, seeking fresh perspectives on game situations, and remaining open to innovative approaches.

Imagine a tennis umpire who, instead of simply applying rules by rote, constantly questions why certain interpretations exist and how they might be used in novel situations. These officials don't just know the rules; they understand the spirit behind them and can adapt to new challenges with confidence and creativity.

Cultivating curiosity involves four key elements: regularly questioning assumptions, studying rule interpretations deeply, seeking new perspectives on game situations, and staying open to innovative approaches. These practices are essential for developing a dynamic and evolving understanding of officiating beyond mere rule application.

The Advantage

Officials who master the art of cultivating curiosity often demonstrate superior adaptability in new or unusual game situations. By constantly questioning and exploring, these officials develop a deeper understanding of the game, allowing them to make more nuanced and accurate decisions.

Curious officials stay more engaged and motivated in their roles. The constant pursuit of knowledge and new perspectives keeps the job fresh and exciting, even after years of experience. This engagement often translates to improved on-field performance and greater job satisfaction.

Another key advantage is improved problem-solving skills. Officials who cultivate curiosity are more likely to think creatively when faced with challenging situations, drawing on their broad knowledge base to find effective solutions. This ability to think outside the box can be crucial in maintaining fair play and managing complex game dynamics.

Importantly, officials who embrace curiosity often become leaders and innovators within the officiating community. Their willingness to question established norms and explore new ideas can improve officiating practices, benefiting the profession.

The Penalty

Officials who neglect to cultivate curiosity may find themselves stuck in rigid thinking patterns, applying rules without fully understanding their purpose or considering alternative interpretations. This inflexibility can lead to poor decision-making in complex or unusual game situations.

These officials can struggle to adapt to changes in the sport or evolving officiating standards. They might resist new techniques or technologies without a curious mindset, potentially falling behind their peers regarding skills and knowledge.

Officials who don't question assumptions or seek new perspectives may also miss opportunities for personal growth and improvement. They might repeat the same mistakes or ineffective practices, unaware of alternative approaches to enhance their performance.

A lack of curiosity can also lead to decreased satisfaction over time. Without the intellectual stimulation from continuous learning and exploration, officiating may begin to feel routine or monotonous, potentially leading to burnout or disengagement.

The Game Plan

To cultivate curiosity and enhance your officiating performance, adopt the following practical strategies:

1. *Create a curiosity journal.* This should be a dedicated notebook or digital document where you regularly record questions, observations, and insights about officiating. Set aside some time after each game or training session to write down:
- One aspect of the game or rules that you want to explore further
- A situation that challenged your understanding or application of the rules
- An idea or approach you'd like to investigate

Review your journal weekly, choosing one topic to research more deeply.

2. *The rule of the week practice.* Each week, select one rule or aspect of officiating to study in depth. This might involve:
- Reading official interpretations and case studies
- Discussing the rule with colleagues or mentors
- Watching game footage to see how the rule is applied in various situations

Share your findings with fellow officials through informal discussions or by presenting at local officiating meetings.

3. *Adopt the cross-sports approach.* Regularly expose yourself to officiating practices from other sports or levels of play. This could involve:
- Attending a clinic or workshop for a different sport
- Shadowing an official in another league or level
- Reading officiating materials from various sports

Look for ideas or approaches that could be adapted to your officiating.

Imagine you're a basketball referee who wants to improve the flow and pace of play. Your curiosity journal notes questions about how other sports manage game tempo. For your rule of the week, you study the mechanics and intent behind the shot clock rules.

Using the cross-sports approach, you attend a hockey officiating clinic and observe how referees manage the nature of their sport. You then reflect on how some techniques, such as positioning or communication strategies, can be adapted to basketball to keep the game moving smoothly.

By consistently applying these strategies, you'll develop a habit of curiosity that continually enhances your officiating skills. The goal isn't to question everything for the sake of it but to develop a deeper, more nuanced understanding of your role and the game you officiate.

As you master this principle, you'll likely find your officiating more dynamic and adaptable. Your ability to question assumptions, seek new perspectives, and stay open to innovative approaches will improve your on-field performance and contribute to your growth as a thoughtful and respected official.

Cultivating curiosity is an ongoing process. Each game, rule study session and conversation with a colleague is an opportunity to learn and grow. Embrace this inquisitive approach, knowing that with each question asked and each new perspective gained, you'll become a more insightful, effective, and valuable member of the officiating community.

RULE 12.2

PRACTICING GRATITUDE—FINDING POSITIVITY

THE CALL

Maintaining a positive outlook is crucial for resilience and performance. This principle focuses on gratitude, emphasizing the importance of starting each game with thankfulness, finding value in every assignment, acknowledging those who support your journey, and celebrating the privilege of serving the game.

Imagine a football referee who, before each match, takes a moment to reflect on the opportunity to officiate, the support of their family, and the chance to contribute to the sport they love. This mindset enhances their personal well-being and influences their approach to the game, fostering a sense of purpose and fulfillment.

Practicing gratitude involves four key elements: beginning each game with a thankful mindset, recognizing the value in every officiating assignment, acknowledging the support of others, and celebrating the privilege of officiating. These practices are essential for maintaining a positive outlook and enhancing job satisfaction.

THE ADVANTAGE

Officials who master the practice of gratitude often experience increased resilience and stress management, as focusing on what they're thankful for helps mitigate the negative impacts of pressure and criticism. This positive mindset can lead to better on-field performance and decision-making.

These officials tend to have a more fulfilling officiating experience. They find value in every assignment and enthusiastically and purposefully approach each game, regardless of its perceived importance. This attitude can lead to greater job satisfaction and a more sustainable career.

Practising gratitude also fosters improved relationships with colleagues and supporters. When you express gratitude for the support you receive, you often build stronger, more supportive networks. This can lead to more opportunities for growth and development and a sense of belonging within the officiating community.

Officials who practice gratitude often demonstrate a deeper appreciation for their role in the sport. This appreciation can lead to a greater sense of responsibility and commitment to excellence, enhancing their overall performance and contribution to the game.

THE PENALTY

Neglecting the practice of gratitude may lead to challenges that can undermine your well-being and effectiveness. You might focus more on the stresses and difficulties of officiating, potentially leading to burnout or decreased job satisfaction over time.

You may also struggle to maintain a positive outlook, especially when faced with criticism or difficult games. Without a grateful mindset, you might become more reactive to negative feedback, eroding your confidence and resilience.

Officials who don't acknowledge the support they receive may also miss out on opportunities for personal growth and stronger relationships within the officiating community. By not expressing gratitude, they might not foster a supportive network to help them navigate challenges and celebrate successes.

Failing to celebrate the privilege of officiating, may result in losing sight of the broader purpose and fulfillment of serving the sport. This can lead to disconnection from the game and your role within it.

The Game Plan

To develop a practice of gratitude and enhance your officiating experience, focus on implementing a straightforward yet powerful approach.

1. *Create a pre-game gratitude ritual.* Before each game, reflect on what you're thankful for. This might include:
- The opportunity to officiate
- The support of family or colleagues
- The chance to contribute to the sport

Write these reflections down in a gratitude journal, or take a moment to acknowledge them silently.

2. *Implement the value in every assignment mindset.* Regardless of the game's perceived importance, approach each assignment with purpose and enthusiasm. Remember that every game is an opportunity to improve, learn, and contribute to the sport.

Imagine you're a lacrosse official preparing for a high school game. As part of your pre-game gratitude ritual, you take a few deep breaths and reflect on what you're thankful for: the opportunity to officiate, the support of your family, and the chance to help young athletes develop their skills.

During the game, you maintain a positive attitude and focus on the value of every assignment. Afterward, you text your mentor quickly, thanking them for their guidance and support throughout the season.

By consistently applying these strategies, you'll develop a mindset of gratitude that enhances your officiating experience and overall well-being. Remember, gratitude isn't just about feeling thankful; it's about cultivating a positive outlook that supports your resilience and performance.

As you master this principle, you'll likely find your officiating career more fulfilling and enjoyable. Your ability to approach each game with gratitude will improve your on-field performance and contribute to a more positive and supportive officiating community.

Practicing gratitude is a skill that improves with practice. Embrace this approach, knowing that with each expression of gratitude, you're not just improving your officiating journey but contributing to a more appreciative and resilient community of officials.

RULE 12.3

CONTINUOUS LEARNING AND GROWTH—THE JOURNEY NEVER ENDS

The Call

Stagnation is the enemy of excellence. This principle emphasizes the importance of continuous learning and growth, exploring different officiating techniques, learning from other sports' methods, investigating the reasoning behind rules, and embracing a performance mindset that views every challenge as an opportunity.

Imagine a soccer referee who stays updated on the latest changes in their sport, studies basketball officiating techniques to manage player interactions, applies rugby's advantage rule concept to enhance game flow, and constantly questions why certain rules exist to understand their application better. This official isn't just keeping up; they're actively pushing the boundaries of their knowledge and skills.

Continuous learning and growth involve four key elements: exploring various officiating techniques, learning from other sports, investigating the rationale behind rules, and maintaining a performance mindset. These practices are essential for developing a dynamic and evolving approach to officiating that adapts to new challenges and continually improves.

The Advantage

Officials who master the art of continuous learning and growth gain several significant benefits. Their broad knowledge base allows them to approach situations from multiple angles, demonstrating their adaptability and problem-solving skills. This versatility can lead to more effective game management and decision-making.

These officials stay more engaged and motivated in their roles. The constant pursuit of knowledge and skill development keeps the job fresh and exciting, even after years of experience. This engagement often translates to enhanced on-field performance and greater job satisfaction.

Increased credibility and respect within the officiating community is another key advantage. Officials known for their commitment to learning and growth are often seen as leaders and innovators, which can lead to more opportunities for advancement and influence within the profession.

When you embrace continuous learning and growth, you are better equipped to handle sports' evolving nature. As rules change, new technologies emerge, and player behaviors evolve, you are ready to adapt and excel in changing environments.

The Penalty

Neglecting continuous learning and growth may hinder your effectiveness and career progression. You might fall behind, struggling to adapt to new rules, technologies, or game dynamics. This can lead to decreased performance and potentially fewer opportunities for high-level assignments.

Furthermore, you may experience a decline in job satisfaction over time. Officiating can become routine or monotonous without stimulating new learning and growth, potentially leading to burnout or disengagement.

Officials who don't explore different techniques or learn from other sports may also miss out on valuable insights that could enhance their performance. They might continue using less effective methods simply because they haven't been exposed to alternatives.

Lastly, a lack of continuous learning can lead to a fixed mindset, where challenges are seen as threats rather than growth opportunities. This mindset can limit an official's resilience and ability to bounce back from mistakes or criticism.

The Game Plan

By implementing the following strategies to continuous learning and growth, you will enhance your officiating performance.

1. *Create a learning action plan.* At the beginning of each season, set three specific learning goals:
- A technique you want to master or improve
- A concept from another sport you wish to explore and potentially adapt
- A rule or aspect of the game you want to investigate more deeply

Break each goal down into actionable steps and set deadlines for achieving them.

2. *Implement the cross-sport study practice.* Each month, choose an officiating technique or concept from a different sport to study. This might involve:
- Watching videos of officials in other sports
- Reading rulebooks or officiating manuals from different games
- Discussing techniques with officials from other sports

Reflect on how these insights might apply to your officiating and experiment with adapting them in your games.

Imagine you're a netball umpire looking to improve your court presence and player management. In your learning action plan, you set a goal to master the art of preventive officiating. For your cross-sports study, you examined how soccer referees use positioning and non-verbal communication to manage player behavior.

Consistently applying these strategies leads to continuous learning and growth habits that enhance your officiating skills and adaptability. The goal isn't just to accumulate knowledge but to apply it creatively to improve your officiating.

As you master this principle, you'll likely find your officiating more dynamic and effective. Your ability to draw from a wide range of techniques, adapt concepts from other sports, and deeply understand the rules will improve your on-court performance and contribute to your growth as a thoughtful and innovative official.

Each game, study session, and conversation with a colleague is an opportunity to learn and improve. Embrace this performance mindset, knowing that with each new insight and skill you develop, you're becoming a more versatile, effective, and valuable member of the officiating community.

BONUS RULE

HOLISTIC WELL-BEING—BALANCING LIFE AND SPORT

The Call

In the demanding world of sports officiating, maintaining holistic well-being is not just beneficial—it's essential. This principle focuses on nurturing overall health and balance, emphasizing the importance of practicing mindfulness, maintaining healthy boundaries, and seeking support when needed. It's about recognizing that peak performance on the field is intrinsically linked to well-being off the field.

Imagine a tennis umpire who starts each match with a brief mindfulness exercise, effectively separates their officiating role from their personal life, and isn't afraid to reach out to colleagues or professionals when facing challenges. This official isn't just surviving the job pressures; they're thriving within it.

Holistic well-being involves three key elements: practicing mindfulness (whistle with awareness), maintaining boundaries (leave the game on the field), and seeking support when needed (strength in seeking support). These practices are essential for sustaining a long, fulfilling officiating career while maintaining personal health and happiness.

The Advantage

Officials who master holistic well-being often demonstrate improved focus and decision-making during games, as mindfulness practices enhance their ability to stay present and aware. This heightened awareness can lead to more accurate calls and better game management.

These officials also tend to experience less stress and burnout. By maintaining clear boundaries between their officiating role and personal life, they can better manage the emotional demands of the job. This balance often translates to increased longevity in their officiating careers and overall life satisfaction.

Improved resilience is another key advantage. Officials who prioritize their well-being and seek support when needed are better equipped to handle the challenges and pressures of officiating. They can bounce back more quickly from difficult games or criticism, maintaining their confidence and effectiveness.

Importantly, officials who embrace holistic well-being often serve as positive role models within the officiating community. Their approach to balancing the demands of officiating with personal health can inspire and guide others, contributing to a healthier, more sustainable officiating culture.

The Penalty

Officials who neglect holistic well-being may face challenges that undermine their performance and quality of life. They might experience higher levels of stress and anxiety, both during games and in their personal lives. This chronic stress can lead to decreased performance, impaired decision-making, and potentially health issues over time.

They may also struggle with burnout or losing passion for officiating. Without clear boundaries, the job pressures can bleed into personal time, leading to resentment or fatigue. This can result in decreased job satisfaction and potentially early exit from officiating.

Officials who don't practice mindfulness or seek support when needed may also be more reactive to criticism or challenging situations. This reactivity can lead to poor on-field decisions or conflicts with players, coaches, or colleagues.

Lastly, by not prioritizing holistic well-being, these officials may miss out on the full potential of their officiating careers. They might not experience the deep satisfaction and personal growth that can come from a balanced, mindful approach to officiating.

The Game Plan

To develop holistic well-being and enhance your officiating experience, focus on implementing the following practical strategies:

1. *Create a mindfulness routine.* Before each game, take 5 minutes to center yourself:
- Find a quiet space and sit comfortably.
- Close your eyes and focus on your breath.
- Mentally scan your body, releasing any tension.
- Set an intention for the game (e.g., "I will officiate with clarity and fairness").

Practice this routine consistently to develop your ability to whistle with awareness.

2. *Implement a post-game boundary ritual.* After each game:
- Take a few deep breaths
- Mentally "pack away" the game's events
- Change out of your officiating uniform
- Engage in a non-officiating activity you enjoy

This ritual helps you leave the game on the field, separating your officiating role from your personal life.

3. *Create a support network map.* Identify at least three sources of support:
- A trusted colleague or mentor in officiating
- A friend or family member outside of officiating
- A professional resource (e.g., counselor, sports psychologist)

Commit to seeking strength in support at least once a month or more frequently when facing challenges.

Imagine you're a volleyball referee preparing for a high-stakes playoff game. You start by practicing mindfulness, centering yourself, and intending to officiate clearly and fairly. During the game, you stay present and aware, making confident decisions.

After the game, regardless of how it went, you engage in your post-game boundary ritual. You change out of your uniform and meet a friend for dinner, shifting your focus to personal time.

The next day, you reflect on the game and decide to contact your officiating mentor from your support network map to discuss a challenging call and seek advice on improving in the future.

Through consistent application of these strategies, you'll develop a holistic approach to well-being that enhances your officiating performance and overall quality of life. This principle equips you with the tools to handle the pressures of officiating and find fulfillment and growth through the experience.

As you master this principle, you'll likely find your officiating career more sustainable and rewarding. Your ability to maintain mindfulness, set healthy boundaries, and seek support when needed will improve your on-field performance and contribute to a more balanced and fulfilling life overall.

Holistic well-being is an ongoing practice. Each game, interaction, and day is an opportunity to nurture your overall health and balance. Embrace this approach, knowing that by taking care of yourself, you'll become a better official and more resilient, satisfied, and effective individual both on and off the field.

RULE 12 IN SUMMARY
THE THRIVE IN OFFICIATING RULE

Think of these four principles as puzzle pieces that fit together to help officials not just survive but thrive in their roles, embracing challenges as opportunities for growth and maintaining well-being:

Rule 12.1. Cultivating curiosity: Encourages officials to maintain an inquisitive mindset by questioning assumptions, studying rules deeply, seeking new perspectives, and remaining open to innovative approaches. This drives continuous improvement and adaptability.

Rule 12.2. Practicing gratitude: Focuses on fostering a positive outlook by starting each game with thankfulness, finding value in every assignment, acknowledging support, and celebrating the privilege of officiating. Gratitude enhances resilience and job satisfaction.

Rule 12.3. Continuous Learning: Highlights the importance of ongoing development by exploring different techniques, learning from other sports, investigating the reasoning behind rules, and embracing challenges as opportunities for growth.

Bonus Rule. Holistic well-being: Promotes mindfulness, maintaining healthy boundaries between officiating and personal life, and seeking support when needed to ensure overall wellness for a sustainable officiating career.

Let's think about how these rules could be applied across different sports:
Rugby
A referee uses curiosity (Rule 12.1) to explore new positioning techniques for better game flow. They start each match with gratitude (Rule 12.2), reflecting on the privilege of officiating. Continuous learning (Rule 12.3) leads them to adapt strategies from rugby's advantage rule to enhance decision-making. Holistic well-being (Rule 12.4) helps them manage stress through mindfulness exercises before games.

Soccer
An official applies curiosity (Rule 12.1) by studying how soccer referees manage player interactions. Gratitude (Rule 12.2) keeps them motivated during long seasons by focusing on the value of each assignment. Continuous learning (Rule 12.3) inspires them to refine their preventive officiating techniques, while holistic well-being (Rule 12.4) ensures they maintain work and personal life boundaries.

Tennis
An umpire embraces curiosity (Rule 12.1), questioning how rules can be interpreted creatively in unique situations. Practicing gratitude (Rule 12.2) helps them stay positive during challenging matches. Continuous learning (Rule 12.3) encourages them to study officiating methods from team sports to improve communication skills. Holistic well-being (Rule 12.4) ensures they stay centered post-match through mindfulness routines.

In each case, the four principles work together:
- Cultivating curiosity opens a door to continuous growth and adaptability
- Practicing gratitude builds a foundation of positivity and resilience
- Continuous learning fuels progress with new insight and techniques
- Holistic well-being creates a safety net that sustains success

When all elements align, you create an environment where you adapt quickly to new challenges with confidence and creativity, resilience is strengthened through gratitude and positivity during adversity, growth is continuous, ensuring skills are refined and expanded over time, and personal well-being is prioritized alongside professional excellence.

Remember: Don't just get through the challenge; learn to thrive within it.

To implement the learnings from Rule 12 – The Thrive in Officiating Rule – Learning from Others Rule, download your bonus copy of *The Whistle Blower Workbook*.
Scan this QR code or visit:

CONCLUSION

ELEVATING EXCELLENCE IN OFFICIATING

As we conclude our journey through the *Whistle Blower: The Mental Toughness Rulebook for Referees, Umpires, and Sports Officials,* it's clear that the path to excellence in officiating is not just about mastering the big moments but also about achieving the small ones. The concept of "one percenter" reminds us that the accumulation of tiny improvements—each seemingly insignificant—can transform a good official into a great one.

The Power of One-Percenters

In officiating, one-percenters are the small, often unnoticed actions that significantly impact the quality of officiating and the overall game management. These include:

Preparation and attention to detail: Thorough pre-game preparation, including studying team tactics and ensuring equipment is in top condition, lays the groundwork for confidence and authority on the field.

Communication skills: Clear verbal commands and effective body language are crucial for maintaining order and respect during games.

Positioning and movement: Optimal positioning to observe play without interfering and anticipating play development to stay ahead of the action are key to making accurate decisions.

Decision-making: Quick, confident decisions in split-second situations, combined with consistency in applying rules throughout the match, are hallmarks of a skilled official.

Game management: Subtle interventions to prevent conflicts from escalating and maintain the appropriate tempo and flow of the game to ensure a smooth and enjoyable competition.

Emotional control: Remaining calm under pressure from players, coaches, and spectators while projecting confidence and authority without appearing arrogant is essential for maintaining respect.

Continuous improvement: Self-reflection and analysis after each match, as well as seeking feedback and learning from experienced colleagues, foster ongoing growth and development.

These one-percenters are not just about individual improvement; they collectively enhance the integrity and enjoyment of the game. By focusing on these small details, officials can elevate their performance, earning respect and contributing to a fairer, more engaging competition.

The Journey to Excellence

As we began this journey, we imagined standing at the center of a roaring stadium, whistle in hand, with thousands of eyes scrutinizing every move. The weight of the game rests on your shoulders, and in a split second, you must make a decision that could change everything.

This is the world of sports officiating, where mental toughness isn't just an advantage—it's a necessity.

Through the 12 rules outlined in this book, we've explored the psychological tools and techniques that separate good officials from great ones. We've delved into strategies for maintaining focus under pressure, techniques for managing on-field conflicts, and methods for building unshakeable confidence. Each rule builds upon the last, creating a comprehensive mental toughness framework tailored specifically for sports officials.

Final Thoughts

As you close this book, remember that the journey to becoming a great official is ongoing. It's about embracing the small improvements that add up to make a significant difference. The one percenters are not just about officiating; they're about building habits of excellence that can benefit every aspect of your life.

In the words of the Japanese proverb, "Fall seven times, stand up eight." This resilience, combined with the pursuit of small but meaningful improvements, distinguishes those who merely officiate from those who truly excel.

As you embark on this journey of continuous improvement, remember that your performance as a referee directly reflects your mental skills. The decisions you make, the composure you maintain, and the respect you command all stem from the strength of your mind.

Prepare to transform how you officiate and approach challenges in all aspects of life. Welcome to the world of mental toughness for referees—where the most important calls are the ones you make inside your head.

The Whistle Blower Workbook: Your Next Step

Designed to help you implement these principles and one-percenters into your officiating practice, *The Whistle Blower Workbook* is available as a free eBook with this book or as a physical copy for purchase. The workbook provides practical exercises and reflection prompts to help you apply the rules and one-percenters in real-world scenarios.

Whether you're a seasoned official or just starting out, the workbook offers a structured approach to developing your mental toughness and refining your skills. It's a tool for turning theory into practice, ensuring that each game is an opportunity to grow, learn, and excel. To download your bonus copy of *The Whistle Blower Workbook*, scan the QR code overpage or visit: https://books.drjolukins.com/tn2elyoas6

BONUS OFFER

WINNING AT WELLBEING: THE MENTAL FITNESS BLUEPRINT

Download your BONUS e-book of Winning at Wellbeing, a mental fitness blueprint for your officiating journey. Scan the QR code or visit: https://books.drjolukins.com/tzgyllnm6p

ABOUT DR. JO

Dr. Jo is often referred to as the psychological Indiana Jones of success! With over twenty-five years in the realm of sports psychology, she's on a quest to uncover the secrets behind peak performance. She finds joy in running with friends (then drinking coffee with them), going on adventures with her husband and two sons, and reading and watching whatever sport she can!
You can connect with Dr. Jo at www.drjolukins.com

facebook.com/DrJoLukins
instagram.com/dr_jo_lukins
linkedin.com/in/drjolukins
youtube.com/@drjolukins

A NOTE FROM DR. JO

If you enjoyed The Whistle Blower, I'd appreciate you sharing your views so others can benefit from your insights.

Leaving a review - whether on Amazon, Goodreads, your place of purchase, or your social media—helps more people discover the book and learn further in their officiating journey.

I'd love to read your feedback! Please email me the link or a message to say hello at excel@drjolukins.com

Thank you for helping elevate the conversation in sport and performance,

Dr Jo Lukins

STAY CONNECTED WITH DR. JO

Elevate your personal and professional game with The Locker Room's positive psychology insights. Dr. Jo presents offers avenues of connection through a weekly podcast 🎧 Tune into The Locker Room; and an insightful monthly newsletter 📖 Sign up for the newsletter & receive your *free* Confidence Checklist

The Locker Room Podcast

Confidence Checklist + Newsletter

READ MORE WITH DR. JO

THE FOLLOWING BOOKS BY DR JO ARE AVAILABLE AT www.drjolukins.com or your favorite online or physical book store.

The Elite: Think like an Athlete, Succeed like a Champion, 2019

In the Grandstands: The Sporting Parents Guide to Raising a Confident & Happy Teens, 2020

The Game Plan: Your 5-month Coaching Program to Champion High-Performance Habits, 202

The Elite and The Game Plan 2-in-1 Book: Champion your Success with Elite Habits, 2023

Belief: Building Unshakeable Confidence, 2024

The Whistle Blower: The Mental Toughness Rulebook for Referees and Umpires, 2025

The Whistle Blower Workbook: The Mental Toughness Workbook for Referees and Umpires, 2025

www.ingramcontent.com/pod-product-compliance
Lightning Source LLC
Chambersburg PA
CBHW060352080526
44583CB00012B/276